INTERPRETING YOUR CHILD'S DRAWINGS AND HANDWRITING

INTERPRETING YOUR CHILD'S DRAWINGS
AND
HANDWRITING
TODDLER TO TEEN

CLAUDE SANTOY

Robson Books

First published in Great Britain in 1992 by
Robson Books Ltd, Bolsover House,
5-6 Clipstone Street, London W1P 7EB

Copyright © 1991 Paragon House
Publishers
The right of Paragon House Publishers to be
identified as author of this work has been
asserted by them in accordance with the
Copyright, Designs and Patents Act 1988

Editorial development by Barbara Brooks

British Library Cataloguing-in-Publication Data
A catalogue record for this book is available
from the British Library

ISBN 0 86051 805 1

Printed by the Guernsey Press Ltd.,
Guernsey, Channel Islands.

CONTENTS

♦

◆ ——————— ◆
PART THREE
◆ ——————— ◆

PRACTICAL APPLICATIONS

INTRODUCTION

♦

This book will help you—as a parent, educator, or interested adult—get to know the children in your life better. If you know many children, you know that they are not miniature adults. Instead, children mature through specific stages of physical, intellectual, and emotional growth. If properly interpreted at each stage, their doodles, drawings, and handwriting reveal surprising and accurate details about their personalities, health, and hidden talents.

Both children and adults reveal their feelings, inhibitions, and anxieties in their doodles and handwriting. Our thoughts and emotions are mirrored in our graphic expression. And because children are constantly growing and changing, aspects of their writing and drawing can change suddenly. Analyzing their graphics calls for a looser, more indulgent interpretation than an adult's hand does. And many strokes, shapes, and slants carry different connotations depending on the age of the writer. My method for analyzing children's handwriting and drawings is both the result of many years of applied research and a natural extension of the technique for interpreting adult handwriting presented in my book, *The ABCs of Handwriting Analysis.*

Your initiation, in Part One, includes a primer on the graphologist's tools and techniques and the kinds of information graphic analysis yields to the practiced eye. In Part Two, you will learn to proceed by analogy through more than 200 samples from many different children between the ages of 2 and 18, which illustrate each chapter. Parents and other child development ex-

perts recognize many stages and age-groups from toddler to teen. Here I impose a scheme which accounts for
no particular theory of child development but rather for
the range of behavior we can observe among children of
the same age—say, 9 year olds—and among children in
the same age-group—the years from 12 to 15, for example. Each chapter begins with a general description of
behaviors typical within each age-group.

As you review the practical applications in Part
Three and try your own hand at the practice tests at the
end of the book, you'll be surprised at how quickly you
begin to apply your new skill and by how helpful graphology can be in keeping up with what's going on in
your child's life. You will also be surprised by the
accuracy of your discoveries concerning your child's
personality.

PART ONE

INITIATION

1

The Graphologist's Tools and Terms

Nowadays, graphology is being put into practice all over the world. Businesses, governments, and individuals hire graphologists to analyze applicants' handwriting samples as an aid to determining their aptitudes, personality traits, or suitability for careers or jobs. On a personal level, graphologists can interpret samples from friends or acquaintances to gauge their compatibility, integrity, or state of mind.

Graphology is not magic. It is rather a science based on observation and analogy. By observing and interpreting a wide variety of samples, pioneers in handwriting analysis have laid the base for anyone to acquire this skill, not as a means of sitting in judgment but rather as a means to better understanding among people. This goal of understanding is paramount in applying graphology to the interpretation of children's drawings and handwriting.

Psychologists tell us that children are born with "temperaments," or predispositions, that combine with early experience to foreshadow their adult personalities. No one can predict the adult character of a person in such a way, though. The child's character is developing continually. Changes take place suddenly, much faster than in the life of an adult. Graphic expression, first in the form of doodles and scribbles and later in the form of drawings and handwriting, likewise changes quickly throughout childhood.

Toddlers and young children draw for their own enjoyment and to communicate with adults, each child with a characteristic flair. Observing a child's graphic output over time provides both a snapshot of the child's inner state at any moment and a fascinating album that charts the overall course of that child's development. You'll be able to spot aberrations and trends, growth spurts and growing pains. Graphology offers extra help in spotting problems or traumas and some coaching on how you might best help your child solve problems and overcome obstacles to healthy character development.

Your primary tool is your flexibility in constantly keeping in mind the changes your child is going through as well as the context of those changes—the way the child relates to experience as well as the experiences themselves. All children are impressionable and easily influenced by their environments. Some children are emotionally fragile; some are stubborn; some are moody. The same child may be timid at one time and boisterous at another, happy or sad, carefree or preoccupied.

Before we begin to analyze the graphic expression of children by studying actual samples, this chapter and the next will provide your initiation into graphology by teaching you how to interpret your children's drawings and handwriting samples. Here are the tools you need and a Glossary of the terms graphologists use to analyze samples.

Tools

Ruler

You will use a ruler to measure the size of the letters, as well as the spelling and the margins. You will also need it to evaluate the "basic line" of the writing. The baseline can be straight, slightly wavy, or extremely wavy. Even the experienced graphologist uses a ruler, because the evaluation of the baseline is crucial and its appearance can be misleading. Our unaided perception is not always correct.

Protractor

In the beginning you will use a protractor to measure the slant, a crucial point in handwriting analysis. After a few exercises, and certainly by the time you have learned my method, you will manage without it.

Magnifying glass

Necessary throughout your career as an amateur or professional graphologist, a magnifying glass will help you detect the less conspicuous aspects of the handwriting before you. A magnifying glass will help you detect evidence of the slightest shaking or trembling of the subject's hand, any unnecessary punctuation, or tiny hidden hooks or retouches otherwise invisible to the naked eye.

A Glossary of Terms

In the beginning you will find yourself referring often to this Glossary, but as you study more samples, you will get a feel for each term and its corresponding stroke. Later on you will consult the Glossary only for exact meanings or shades of meaning.

Remember once again that flexibility is the watchword: Often several meanings are given for one term, but all meanings do not apply in all cases. In each sample there is an interplay of individual signs and strokes. Only in the context of the entire sample can an analysis or interpretation be made. An isolated sign gives no information. Likewise an interpretation is an opinion, not a fact. As your knowledge grows, your skills will improve, and you will learn to make the right choice among the possibilities.

◆

Altered strokes

The writer goes back to finished words and tries to improve some of the letters, often for no reason. As a result, some letters may become difficult to recognize. You may need your magnifying glass to analyze the strokes.

adult

no Smoker

child

Once that
liked to

MEANING: **Adult**—perfectionism, hypocrisy, deceit-fulness, obsessiveness, fear, anguish, anxiety.

Child—timidity; humility; feelings of infe-riority, anxiety, anguish, or depres-sion; possible tendencies toward self-absorption, spelling difficulties, eating problems.

◆

Angular strokes

Sharp angles in letters and connecting strokes prevail. Although angles are rare in children's handwriting, similar angles can appear in their doodles and draw-ings, as we'll see later on, and mean the same as in handwriting.

adult

Thanks

child

Luniane.

MEANING: **Adult**—decisiveness, ambition, aggressive-ness, pragmatism, materialism, viril-ity, energy; harshness, selfishness, cru-elty, violence (when angular hooks are seen), greed.

Child—fast thinking pattern, lively mind, quick, understanding; virility, irrita-bility, aggressiveness; trying to break free from inner tensions.

◆

Arcades

Tops of letters very rounded; archlike links among letters, words, or other strokes; arches in capital letters.

adult

child

MEANING: **Adult**—vanity, arrogance, deceitfulness, manipulativeness; lingering feelings of inferiority.

Child—humility, obedience, application; when seen in the writing of the adolescent, slightly immature and selfish.

◆

Backward slant (reversed, sinistrogyric)

Handwriting leans to the left. In a sample from a left-handed person there is no particular meaning, nor is there any negative connotation when found in children's handwriting. Note especially in analyzing samples from adolescents, that a backward slant may occur spontaneously from time to time in children from 12 to 18. After 18, usually suddenly, the backward slant disappears.

adult *Same*

child *writing to tell you for breakfirst. First corn flakes, Eggs*

MEANING: **Adult**—immaturity, egocentricity, stubbornness; general lack of spontaneity; unresolved past problems, such as excessive attachment to the mother. This person can be deceitful as a friend and untrustworthy at work. Inner anxiety can prompt lying and "dissembling" or putting on a false face—that is, disguising or concealing facts, intentions, or feelings.

Child—ability to concentrate and the tendency to think before acting; not impulsive, rather timid, sometimes inhibited. Remember the backward slant has no significance in the handwriting of children, and its appearance in the age-groups from 12 to 18 is normal. Usually this slant disappears suddenly.

♦

Baseline

When you place your ruler beneath the lines of a writing sample, you will find the baseline, which may be straight or meandering, and may ascend or descend on the page. Children usually write on lined paper, which makes for a straight baseline. Sometimes, in spite of the lines, or when children write on unlined paper, (for example, a postcard) their baselines can meander, ascend, or descend.

The meaning is the same for adults and children.

ascendant

MEANING: Optimism, courage, happy disposition.

◆

descendent

MEANING: Pessimism, depression, poor health; need for care and affection.

◆

slightly meandering

for me here at school.

MEANING: Happy disposition; well-balanced, lively child.

◆

very meandering

So I'm writing This

MEANING: Instability, turbulence, temper tantrums;
the child is difficult and moody.

◆

straight (following the lines of the paper)

servant

MEANING: docile, calm, and well-balanced; the child
tries to comply with the wishes of
parents and teachers.

◆

Clubbed strokes

Irregular pressure. Rarely found in children's handwriting; clubbed strokes can appear in the writing of adolescents.
The meaning is the same for adults and children.

horizontal

Anna Julia

MEANING: Sexual ambivalence that is difficult to re-
press; possible bisexual tendencies.
This person is capable of pushing
friends away—brutally if necessary—
in order to preserve a sense of personal freedom.

♦

vertical

MEANING: Frustrations, obsessiveness, drug or alcohol abuse; physical and mental health
problems. After the age of 18, vertical
clubbed strokes often disappear, as do
the problems that caused them.

♦

Coils

The pen adds useless strokes to the letters. Seen mainly
in *a* and *o* and in beginning and ending strokes. This
phenomenon appears frequently with adolscents; it is
usually temporary.

MEANING: **Adults and to a lesser degree, children—**
egocentric, egotistic, and inhibited
(may indicate sexual fantasies and

acting out); a person who dissembles and lies. In adults, coils reveal business acumen.

◆

Connected script

This is simply the style of handwriting taught at school; therefore, it has no special meaning in a child's handwriting. In adolescents and adults, a very connected script reveals an analytical and deductive mind, mathematically gifted, good visual memory.

adult

and lasts for

child

nine-year-old

◆

Disconnected (juxtaposed) script

Texas is very warm

MEANING: **Adults and children**—good intuition, good auditory memory, glib or talkative, independent. Occasionally signals manual creativity (if the writng is slow and the pressure strong). Consideration for others; sometimes, inner loneliness.

◆

Disconnected and connected script

Some letters within the words are connected and some are disconnected. Usually the person is a speedy writer.

I'll start by explaing hapenings. Last night

MEANING: **Adults and children**—intelligence, cultural refinement, lively or spontaneous, intellectual artistic creativity.

◆

Distorted script

Twisted strokes—use your magnifying glass.

adult

Will allways of you with

child

avoidance behind time in my life

MEANING: **Adult**—various physical and mental illnesses.

Child—thyroid problems; usually temporary. Frequently seen in the script of the adolescent.

◆

Embellished script

Appears more often in children's handwriting than in adult's. As always, when you consider the writing of a child, the meaning is not as strong as for the adult. The embellishments of the child can be temporary and often pass away suddenly.

MEANING: **Adults and to a lesser degree, children—** vain, immature, selfish, dishonest, low intelligence, dissembling.

♦

Forward (progressive) slant

Handwriting leans to the right. Rarely seen in the writing of the very young child, who first learns to print with straight, vertical strokes.

MEANING: **Adults and children—**optimism, ambition, dynamic and happy disposition; passion for a chosen activity, spontaneity.

♦

Garlands

The *m* and *n* are written like *w* or *u*. Rare in children's handwriting. However, similar strokes can be found in their doodles and drawings. The meaning is the same as for the garlands of adults.

and

MEANING: Friendly, sociable, obliging, easily influenced person. Such a child is affectionate and charming.

◆

Inhibited script

Very tight letters, backward slant, extremely large margins.

seen a temple in her sky looked. The Valley of the kegesta along w/ Syrac I stayed. I'm heading tomorrow, today I took a

MEANING: **Adults and children**—inhibited, lacks spontaneity; good concentration; a selfish or avaricious person.

◆

Jumbled script

Letters flow into each other and into other lines. Handwriting is very difficult to read.

storms & strive in silence

MEANING: **Adults and children**—mental confusion, dishonesty, tendency toward psycho-

logical disorder. Denotes alcohol and/
or drug abuse in advanced stages.

◆

Launching upward stroke

adult

child

MEANING: **Adult**—violent temper, difficult to keep in
check; mean and vengeful.

Child—temper tantrums which often disappear at adolescence.

◆

Loops

Found in consonants; do not confuse with coiling
strokes. Loops also appear in doodles and drawings
with the same meaning.

MEANING: **Adults and children**—perseverence: tenacity, willpower, good concentration.

◆

18

Loops in letter *s*

MEANING: a possessive and jealous person.

♦

Monotonous (upright) script

The writing is too perfect and looks too nice. Appears
frequently in the early handwriting of the young child;
should disappear by adolescence.

adult

adolescent

child

MEANING: **Adult and adolescent**—neurotic tendencies.

Child—no special meaning.

♦

19

Overlapping strokes

The writer goes over the same letter several times. Overlapping strokes are typical while children are learning to write and tend to disappear suddenly.

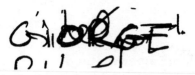

MEANING: **Adults and to a degree, children**—anxiety, lack of spontaneity; dishonesty, dissembling, lying, neurotic tendencies.

♦

Pasty script

Thick, slow, heavy, inkfilled strokes.

their hands, lolling their fat pink mouths & sunshing their tales..

MEANING: **Adult**—hedonism; neurotic tendencies; sloth.

Child—dreamy and lazy; self-absorbed; loss of interest in the surrounding world.

♦

Ringlets in the script

Ringlets appear mainly in *a*, *o*, *n*, and *m*; frequently in doodles and drawings of young children.

George

MEANING: **Adults and children**—charming and seductive; very friendly and sociable;
able to manipulate others.

◆

Round script

Most of the strokes and letters are round; frequently
found in children's handwriting.

Dear Miranda

MEANING: **Adults and children**—extremely affectionate and attached to other people; seductive, hedonistic, appreciates the
pleasures of life.

◆

Spasmodic script

Varying pressure within words. Rare in children's handwriting but can be found in the script of the adolescent.

To George,

MEANING: **Adult and adolescent**—physical or mental
illness; alcohol and/or drug abuse.

Child—rare; no special meaning except,
perhaps, slight nervousness.

◆

Sticklike script

Rare in children's handwriting but can appear in their drawings.

there any real cra
of these sets of she

MEANING: **Adult and adolescent**—cruel, harsh, ruthless; rigid; selfish; in certain cases, neurotic tendencies.

Child—monotonous, sticklike strokes are characteristic of children who are working out aggressive or violent impulses.

♦

Tapered strokes

Letters finish pointed; words diminish in size. Very rare in children's handwriting but can be found in the script of the adolescent.

till

MEANING: **Adults and to a degree, in children**—destructive, caustic humor; a cynical person; if the tapered stroke is vertical, regressive libido. (In graphology, the libido encompasses joy of life, willpower, and sexuality.)

♦

Thread letters and connections

Letters that look like a continuous thread, difficult to distinguish and read.

MEANING: Escapist, timid, inhibited, very nervous and impatient; often signals neurotic behavior.

◆

Unfinished strokes

The handwriting is vague and difficult to read. Letters do not touch the baseline.

adult

child

MEANING: **Adult**—sensitive, impressionable, timid, nervous, vulnerable, diplomatic and capable of lying; suffering from inner anxiety.

Child—timid, inhibited, suffering feelings of inferiority; extremely impressionable and sensitive to scolding.

Summary Table

Use the following table for quick reference as you analyze and interpret children's drawings and handwriting.

In children's handwriting, strokes which are . . .	may indicate . . .
altered	anxiety; younger children are merely perfecting their letters
angular	intelligence, aggressiveness, masculinity
arcades	compliance; selfishness or arrogance in older teens
backward slant	normal/temporary into late adolescence; inhibitions
baseline	clues to disposition
clubbed	ambivalence; rare until adolescence
coils	egocentricity, sexual acting out; appears at puberty
connected	analytical mind
disconnected	intuitive, independent
disconnected & connected	intellectual, artistic
embellished	age-appropriate immaturity; vanity
garlands	friendliness, charm
inhibited	inhibitions; selfishness

In children's handwriting, strokes which are . . .		may indicate . . .
jumbled		mental confusion; substance abuse
launching upward		active temper
loops		perseverance
overlapping		normal as kids learn to write; anxiety; dissembling
pasty		laziness, self-absorption
ringlets		seductiveness, manipulative behavior; sociability
round		affectionate, feminine
sticklike		rare; cruelty, harshness

2

Interpreting Children's Graphic Expression

With tools and terms at hand, you are now ready to begin gathering samples. This chapter explains how to select them. In preparation for analyzing the samples in the following chapters and those in your own collection, you will also discover here how to interpret general elements of graphic expression—layout, size, slant, shape, pressure, and speed.

How to Choose Samples

Select samples from two or three children. Ask the children to use unlined white paper and crayons or ballpoint pen for drawings and handwriting. Felt markers and soft-tip pens have the drawback of not allowing us to study the pressure of the strokes, and therefore to assess the health of the person. Children should write their names and ages on their drawings and sign their handwriting samples. Other information essential to a case history includes the child's sex, grade in school, and number of older and younger siblings. All these factors will influence your interpretations.

The ideal sample is a spontaneous drawing or message written to you personally. Content is not important. Copying a poem or other passage or writing from dictation tend to make the handwriting mechanical and likely will distort your analysis. If an adult has created the sample, you will learn to detect the trick. People who can successfully disguise and imitate handwriting are as rare as successful art forgers.

Be aware that young children like to draw, as a rule, while older children and teenagers may offer you a sample of their handwriting only.

Layout

Children's Written Messages

Always consider the age of your subject. There is no particular significance in the way children use the page. Young children usually use the whole sheet of paper and leave no margins or irregular margins. The more children write, the more they become conscious of margins, how to address envelopes, and the formalities of written correspondence.

Likewise, spacing between letters or words and lines of writing often is irregular. This is natural. However, if the spacing is extremely irregular or the words are jumbled and difficult to read, the child might have psychological problems. The child's background and the context of the message are vital to interpreting such clues.

If the child leaves wide spacing between words, as shown in the following sample, possible interpretations are that he or she has a rather independent character and/or may be feeling a bit lonely:

of December and I shall see you then.

◆

Signatures

The signature has virtually no meaning until late in adolescence. Even then, from the late teens until the early twenties, your interpretations must remain flexible. A signature alone is never sufficient for drawing a clear interpretation. Likewise, a letter with no signature offers less insight into its writer.

As a general rule, you will examine the signature for its relationship to the rest of the message—placement under the text of the message; similarity to the handwriting in the text; presence or absence of paraphs (flourishes) in the signature.

The Layout of a Child's Drawing

The many samples throughout the book will help you to proceed by analogy when you study children's drawings. When they are very young, before they can write, their drawings yield clues to their emerging personalities, as you'll see in these examples:

Example 2.1 The normal, well-balanced, happy child will place the main part of a drawing in the center of the paper. There will be scenery, including animals or people. Some open, white space will be left among them.

Example 2.2   The shy, timid, obedient child who works hard at school to please teachers, parents, and other adults will fill the paper in completely with colors and will often draw houses standing close together. There will be no animals and no people in these drawings.

Example 2.3   The child who is talented and creative but inhibited will use strong colors and a series of angular, monotonous strokes to fill out drawings.

Example 2.4   The child who draws only a few disconnected strokes which are difficult to see as a real picture has problems with concentration and usually is disobedient and boisterous. This child is restless.

◆

Example 2.1
A well-balanced, happy-go-lucky child who is extremely sociable.

◆

Example 2.2
A shy, extremely obedient child who makes efforts to please grown-ups.

◆

Example 2.3
This artistically gifted child has some inhibitions.

◆

Example 2.4
A boisterous, often disobedient child who cannot concentrate and probably feels insecure. (Note the numerous sexual emblems. See page 42 for more information.)

Size

Handwriting

Generally speaking, a child's handwriting is larger than an adult's. The younger the child, the larger the letters. The size of a young child's script most likely depends on the instructions of adults and therefore has little meaning.

As children mature and become more conscientious, their individual handwriting will, as a rule, become smaller. Remember two things:

1. Each child is unique. Compare the sizes of one

child's handwriting at different ages to observe changes.

2. Your complete interpretation will always depend on the child's age-group.

The Size of Children's Drawings

Again, size often depends on the instructions given by adults and the size of the paper. But keep these observations in mind as you analyze the following examples:

Examples 2.5 & 2.6 The well-balanced, happy child who does well at school will use the whole available space and draw familiar surroundings. For instance, a house, a garden, parents or friends, and maybe animals. Usually the people and animals are rather large compared with the houses or the trees. This is normal.

Example 2.7 The timid child will avoid drawing people or make them extremely small, generally without faces or hands.

Example 2.8 Children who are afraid of some adult will draw the feared person with big teeth and long fingers.

Example 2.9 The dreamer, who has a great imagination, draws spaceships, unknown beings, and abstract designs. A dreamy child may be unhappy in the real world and try to escape into an imaginary world.

Example 2.10 The violent child uses large, thick strokes and bold colors, such as red, black, or purple to work out aggression.

♦

32

Ex. 2.5
The happy child.

Ex. 2.6
This boy of 4 is quite happy and lively. He has noticed that babies have large heads compared to the size of their bodies.

Ex. 2.7
The timid child feels insecure.

♦

34

Ex. 2.8
The frightened child.

◆

Ex. 2.9
The dreamer.

◆

Ex. 2.10
The violent child.

◆

A Practice Exercise

From what you know so far—and without looking at my captions for Examples 2.11, 2.12, and 2.13—how would you characterize each drawing? Now look at the captions. Do we agree or disagree?

◆

Ex. 2.11
The unstable or restless child.

◆

Ex. 2.12
The problem child.

◆

Ex. 2.13
This is the drawing of an artistic, dexterous, 6-year-old
girl. The colors are primarily bright blues, reds, greens,
and purple.

Zones

The following sketch-plan of the three principal zones used for adults can also be applied loosely to the handwriting of children and to a lesser degree—like certain terms in the Glossary—to doodles and drawings.

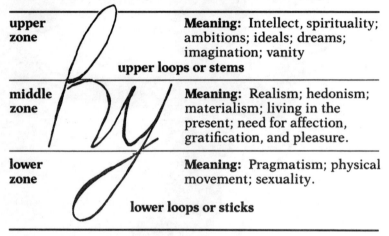

upper zone	**Meaning:** Intellect, spirituality; ambitions; ideals; dreams; imagination; vanity
	upper loops or stems
middle zone	**Meaning:** Realism; hedonism; materialism; living in the present; need for affection, gratification, and pleasure.
lower zone	**Meaning:** Pragmatism; physical movement; sexuality.
	lower loops or sticks

Zones Applied to Handwriting

Pronounced upper or lower loops are very rare in children's handwriting. This makes sense, because pronounced loops indicate deep frustrations in each related zone. Loops may reveal related tendencies or transient frustrations when observed in the handwriting of adolescents, but like other strokes may disappear suddenly.

◆

This person has higher goals and ideals but cannot reach them immediately and so feels frustrated; behavior can show some conceit and lack of respect for other people; vanity.

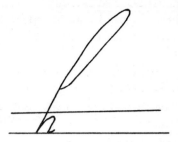

◆

This writer craves physical and material gratification and feels frustrated sexually.

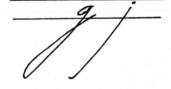

◆

This adolescent feels frustrated in all zones—intellectual, material, and sexual.

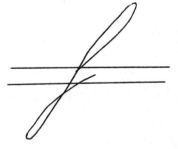

Zones Applied to Doodles

Here are some hints for analyzing the scribbles of children under 4. Consider the placement of the doodles on the paper.

The dreamer   **The affectionate child**   **The boisterous child**

◆

Poor concentration, moody, restless.   **Temper tantrums**

What Shapes Tell Us

Samples of letter shapes and their meanings are pictured in the Glossary. You may want to glance back and review them.

Every individual has both "masculine" and "feminine" traits (that is, traits that have come to be labeled as masculine or feminine by society). When we say that a handwriting sample reveals femininity or many mas-

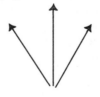

culine traits, we are referring to these cultural labels. The writer we are analyzing can belong to either sex.

The handwriting of a mature, well-balanced adult will contain a mixture of angular (masculine) and round (feminine) strokes, perhaps with added garlands and ringlets. Children generally show a very round or, less often, an angular script. Garlands and ringlets appear mainly in their drawings and mean the same as in adult handwriting: sociability, charm, femininity, seductiveness, manipulative behavior.

The round letters in the following sample reveal that this child is affectionate and charming. Note the garlands and ringlets in the dog's fur.

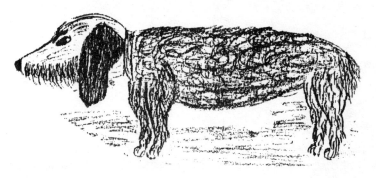

Claude,

Well, I am now at

School, Greshams and I am

Girl of 11.

♦

In the following sample, the child's angular writing shows a sharp mind, wit, quick understanding, and a rather ambitious, tough, masculine character. The angles can also be seen in his drawings. This boy knows what he wants and does not give in easily. He can be impatient, nervous, and is not especially affectionate.

The extreme rightward slant of his handwriting reveals that this child is passionate about his activities or in his feelings. We'll analyze slant in the following section.

Boy of 12.

◆

Sexual Emblems and Shapes

Young children have a natural curiosity about sex. Often they will draw shapes or things that remind us adults of sex. Look again at Example 2.4 on page 30. In Part Two, you will see more sexual emblems in the drawings of toddlers and children.

Lush, round shapes reveal more feminine aspects of character; sharp angles reveal more masculine traits, regardless of the child's sex. Watch for triangular shapes, which indicate energy and sexuality. And note that rectangular shapes reveal manual or technical abilities. Circles often represent imagination and intellect in the drawings of older children.

In general, between the ages of 6 and 12 children's sexuality submerges as they occupy themselves with aspects of intellectual and social/emotional development, which apparently are more pressing during this period. Freud called the period between 6 and 12 "latency," believing that the child's sexual curiosity lay dormant until the onset of adolescence. It's interesting that sexual themes in children's drawings emerge again at puberty and remain throughout the teenage years and beyond. As noted earlier, though, many teens will pass up the opportunity to draw. In later chapters you will learn to identify their emerging sexuality and sexual concerns mainly through their handwriting samples.

What the Slant Tells Us

This general sketch-plan shows how the slant of adult handwriting can be interpreted. It applies to a degree to children's handwriting, depending on age-group.

Monotonous (Upright) script:
Power of concentration and reasoning; discipline; economy; tenacity.

Backward (reversed) slant:
Inhibitions, longing for living in the past, repression and regret, pessimism, stubbornness, deceit, dishonesty.

Forward (Progressive) slant:
Optimism, dynamism, enthusiasm, ambition, spontaneity, sociability, passion.

Samples of these slants appear in the Glossary.

Upright Script

Young children usually learn to write this way.

Thanks

MEANING: The youngster is well balanced and obedient.

◆

In adolescents, upright script looks rigid and monotonous.

for some time in October.
available then, i plan to
would, therefore, appreci
any other period of time
*   I have friends i*
Your bookshop sounds lik

MEANING: The child might exhibit some neurotic tendencies.

◆

The Backward Slant

Contrary to its connotation in adult handwriting, the
backward slant carries no negative meaning in a child's
script. The backward slant appears frequently and fleet-
ingly during adolescence. Samples of children between
6 and 11:

to breakfast and

One day
Sudieney
t hex

denly grabbed the ma
him to the ground. As
led other people grabl
trying to pull him a
the mango the orano
in

MEANING: These children appear timid. Perhaps they are trying to escape reality by fleeing back into the security of the past (Freud would say back into the safety of Mother's womb.)

◆

46

Samples of children from 11 to 17:

*nly just managed to get
fer our breakfast begins
t and I awoke at quatre*

Dear MRS Heggie,

*I am sorry to
you are ill and*

MEANING: A backward slant in the handwriting of the adolescent is normal. This is a period of sudden change, and the phenomenon is only temporary. Usually around 18 the backward slant disappears altogether. If it does not, its meaning grows more negative and is linked to deceit and hypocrisy in the young adult.

♦

The Progressive Slant

You will rarely see a forward slant in the handwriting of children under 12.

please don't worry about OK. I know you must be

MEANING: **Adults and children**—dynamism, ambition, optimism, spontaneity, passion.

♦

Fluctuating Slant

These are varying slants in the same sample or in different samples from the same person.

Dear Claude,
I had English first lesson then Divinity followed by first had French and this

MEANING: **Adults and children**—instability, mood swings, temper tantrums. Remember that in childhood a fluctuating slant can be a transient occurrence.

Pressure

In order to appraise pressure, hold the sample upside down and toward the light. If bulging lines appear, the pressure is heavy. If you can just barely guess that there is a drawing or writing sample on the other side, the pressure is light. Pressure is difficult to judge in samples written in pencil or felt-tip pen. Above all, avoid the analysis of photocopies!

The pressure of a writing sample provides clues to many characteristics, foremost among them the relative health of the writer. Children who tend to be sickly can improve their general health with regular exercise. This will show up as a heavier pressure in their writing and drawing.

Heavy Pressure

It became interes
and exciting agai
believed in me.
had some wonderf

and hope to see you
again sometime,
love

MEANING: **Adults and children**—physically robust and healthy; energetic, ambitious, achievement-oriented, decisive and responsible. Heavy pressure also implies willpower, strong libido, affectionate nature, and dexterity.

♦

Light Pressure

MEANING: **Adults and children**—intelligence, cultural refinement, latent intellectual abilities or creativity, sensitivity. The writer is a romantic and may be impressionable, irritable, or nervous. A sharp quick mind, but often easily influenced; weak libido and precarious health.

♦

Clubbed or Irregular Pressure

You have seen this stroke in the Glossary. However, to learn to proceed by analogy, it's useful to look at many different samples.

MEANING: **Adults and children**—emotional detachment, cut off from reality, possibly the result of frustrations which are difficult to bear, or a problem with drugs or alcohol. Bad health, instability, lack of control; limited reliability, severe restlessness and impatience; possible neurosis or psychosis; lack of logical reasoning.

Speed

Knowing the speed at which a person writes—in combination with your other observations—offers clues to the writer's overall disposition, integrity, intellect, and level of cultural refinement and education. Obviously, speed by itself has little meaning, especially in the handwriting or drawing of children.

Speedy Writing

There are two ways to evaluate speed. The easiest is to watch the child write or draw. If this is not possible, remember that a fairly clear, readable handwriting with a progressive slant and a normal or light pressure can be considered speedy. A connected, garlanded stroke indicates even greater speed. The size is small. As a rule, the older the child, the speedier the script.

*How are you? I am;
I come from Holland!*

child of 13

MEANING: **Adults and children**—quick mind, cultural refinement, intelligence, latent intellectual creativity; impatience, sensitivity, reliability.

◆

Slow Writing

Generally speaking, slow writing is never very positive. Naturally, young children, who are just learning, write slowly. They are perfecting their strokes. In a child under 13, there is no significance. If the child is older, the meaning is the same as for adults. Adults who don't write often also may write slowly. Whether this is significant depends on the interplay of all your observations.

*(we have own own magazine)
distributed to universities
revica. I would now like to*

was not in least incon-vient, I was m

adult

◆

was really nice and lovely tan on my arms so much for doing Pizza's they were

child of 11

MEANING: **Adults**—slow thinker and worker; possibly deceitful; lacking spontaneity and maturity; can behave childishly and unreliably.

PART TWO

SAMPLES

3

The Emerging Child
Toddler to 5

Children love to draw for their own enjoyment. Children who are just learning to talk find that they can also express themselves with paper and crayons. Their scribbles and drawings give us some clues to their emerging personalities.

Interpreting Doodles and Scribbles

Adults and children alike doodle and scribble at any age. It's natural, especially during long lectures or conferences or while we're on the phone. The analysis of our doodles is not far from the following interpretations of the scribbles made by small children.

Toddlers often will start off by drawing circles, large and made slowly at first, then drawn faster and faster toward the center, which will be the darkest area of the scribble. As in handwriting, round shapes imply affection and femininity. Angular strokes show energy and masculinity. As a boy gets older, his drawings become more rectangular and angular. The scribbles of the little girl tend to stay round even when she grows up.

Samples

This boy of 2½ is still very much a baby, extremely egocentric and in need of his mother's affection.

◆

The same boy at the age of 3 tries to draw a picture—some designs appear outside his scribble.

◆

Danielle Is 5

She tries to write. She is perfecting her letters (overlapping strokes). There are garlands and ringlets in the roof of the house and in the clouds, indicating that Danielle is very feminine and charming. She needs a lot of affection and feels a little lonely, as revealed by the widely spaced words; the large, empty space between the house and the sky; and the absence of people.

◆

A Very Lively Boy of 5

The head has a nose, mouth, and eyes. Garland strokes and ringlets—evidence of sociability—design the hair. He uses all the space to tell his story. Everything is related. He is observant, well balanced, and shows a curiosity beyond his years. The sexual symbols are numerous. Look at the shapes!

♦

Another Boy of 5

Not only is he learning his letters but this boy is also writing phonetically ("This is a witch in a castle"). He makes an effort to write well. The child is obviously perseverant, curious, and imaginative. He is appropriately timid and inhibited for his age-group.

◆

Diana Is 5

Her drawings show that she is observant and tries to communicate. At the left, we see that she has noticed that babies' heads are large in proportion to their bodies. She is capable of drawing eyes, nose, and mouth. Hands and feet are added. However, these hands are extremely large, as are the teeth, indicating that Diana may be afraid of someone.

Her drawing at the right illustrates a bird she has

seen in cartoons. She has a latent manual artistic talent, and her sense of humor is acute.

◆

Nancy, 5 Years Old

She cannot write yet, but her drawing reveals that her mind is open and lively. She is obedient and will do well at school, as she is capable of concentrating. Her sense of responsibility is also advanced for her age-group. This healthy and well-balanced little girl shows some maturity.

Her drawing illustrates a whole story. We see her sleeping in her house, eating in the garden, and walking her two dogs. Everything is carefully related to everything else. Her mind is analytical and deductive. We do not see her parents; obviously she is quite independent. Numerous round shapes, garlands, and ringlets indicate her femininity. Nancy is affectionate, organized, and attached to her home.

◆

Charlotte Is 5 Years Old

She has a lively mind and curiosity which are advanced
for her age-group. Her tenacity is obvious: She tries to
write correctly. Considering her age, the meandering
baseline does not have any special meaning, but it is
slightly ascending, like her drawing, which implies a
well-balanced, optimistic child. The slant is unsteady,
and the letters are different sizes, sometimes improved
with covered strokes. All this points to a girl who is
anxious to do well and please her parents. The extremely wide spacing between the words clearly indicates that Charlotte feels a little lonely and wants to be
closer to her parents.

Charlotte.

I am going to Nickys
Party on thursday.
I will enjoy it very
muck. and a Plait in my

hair.

In the drawing, garland strokes illustrating the petti-
coat reveal that Charlotte is sociable and affectionate.
The colors, bright blue and purple, and the monotonous
strokes of her drawings indicate that she may not be a

good eater (See Chapter 8). The superfluous dot after each of her friends's names reveals Charlotte's critical mind. I interpret in this and in the lack of hands and feet in the girls she draws signs of inhibitions and difficulty trusting anyone. The pressure of her strokes in the writing and in the drawing is average to strong, indicating her good physical health.

REMEMBER: All the samples in this book were written and drawn by children. If an adult imitates their writing, the results of the analysis will not be the same. Even beginning graphologists can spot forgeries or imitations easily. Disguising your script is as difficult as duplicating the painting of a Rembrandt.

◆

Olivia Is 5½

She appears healthy, well balanced, happy, and charming (ringlets, garland strokes going upward, fairly strong pressure). She writes well. Olivia has latent manual artistic abilities (strong colors, angular strokes).

Bill Is 6 Years Old

He cannot write yet. Bill appears happy, healthy, and
well balanced. His drawing represents his friends at the
playground. They all have faces with eyes and mouths,
and bodies with hands, arms, and legs. The colors are
pink, orange, yellow, and green; the strokes are mainly
round.

I find the general aspect of this drawing pleasant
but slightly confused. That is, Bill is impatient and does
not like to concentrate on one thing for too long. The
round strokes indicate his need for affection; he still
feels like mother's little baby. Perhaps she spoils her
only child, and this makes him slightly immature.

Aurelia Is 6

She cannot write yet but has great manual abilities. This charming and feminine little girl is perhaps already able to cook several dishes. Aurelia, an only child, has great need for affection, as shown by the many circles in her drawing.

The colors are bright and various, and the pressure is strong. Her strokes are regular and firm. The child is happy, healthy, well balanced. She knows what she wants, and as she also appears rather spoiled, she usually *gets* what she wants!

◆

A Boy Who Is 6

This little boy is extremely curious about sex, which represents a big mystery to him. Note the shapes. The color is red. Pretty normal at this age. The child is happy and well balanced.

A Boy of 6

He is happy, obedient, and well balanced. His masculinity is evident (numerous triangles). The person with the face represents his mother; she appears more important than her three children, who do not seem to represent real people as yet to the boy. They look like babies without any personality—no faces or hands. We can see that he tries to obey (the house has a door, a roof, and windows). The garden around the house indicates that his personality is well integrated.

◆

A Girl Who Is 6

This little girl just started school. She cannot write at all. Her drawing shows a strong pressure and some precise strokes. She is very observant and perseverant. Her bunny is finished and recognizable. This girl is intelligent; she has the ability to represent the rabbit in movement. She has latent artistic gifts.

This child seems well balanced, happy, and very attached to animals. I think that the few weeks she has spent at school have proved satisfactory. She probably pays attention to the teacher, enjoys the lessons, and tries to do well.

◆

Alex Is 6

He is not yet going to school but nevertheless tries to write his name correctly. His drawings prove that in this case—although he goes over each letter twice—this is not done out of anxiety. The child is simply perfecting his letters.

His little man has a smiling face, feet, and hands. The hat seems to be floating above the head, which reveals Alex's optimistic disposition. In the second drawing, note that he draws a house with windows, a door and a handle, a roof with a chimney. His sun has a face and beams, which indicates that Alex is happy, well balanced, and sociable.

Rebekka Is 6

She can write her name. She is very lively and sociable.
She mainly draws people. They all look happy and have
smiling faces. The colors are bright (purple, pink, and
green) and various. The sun is shining. The garland
strokes and the ringlets in the hair and in the sky reveal
both sociability and some manipulative behavior. She
is very charming and feminine, interested in clothes
and fashion. She is healthy and well balanced. She is
attached to her family and craves affection.

John Is 6

He cannot write yet. His bird is easily recognizable. He obviously has some latent artistic skill. However, the strokes representing the feathers are slightly monotonous, and the colors, gray, brown, and a little green for the head, point to a possible psychological fragility.

John is intelligent, perseverant, healthy, and well balanced. He has manual abilities but seems rather shy and sad. Drawing is a good outlet for him.

♦

Peter Is 6 Years Old

He is not yet at school, but he's begun to print words. His mind is analytical. His drawing is meant to tell a science fiction story. He loves cartoons and watches a lot of television. He has a good imagination and a lively mind. His interests are numerous and include natural curiosity about sex (see the sexual emblems).

Peter seems healthy and well balanced. He is tenacious: he finishes the tasks he begins. At times he can be boisterous and stubborn. His aggressiveness comes through in the angular strokes which illustrate the little man flying off toward the cosmos. I think that Peter would like to be grown-up and free.

♦

Sonia Is 6

She cannot write yet, but her drawing is explicit. Sonia is illustrating her taste in fashion and make-up. Garlands and ringlets reveal her charming, feminine character and her need for affection. The many details indicate that she is observant and perseverant. She has imagination. She is mature for her age. Her mind is analytical and deductive; everything is linked together in her sketch. The pressure of her pen is regular and strong. Sonia is in good health, happy, and well balanced.

◆

Mary Is 6

She is perfecting her handwriting. Wide spaces between her words reveal her loneliness. Mary's drawings tell me that she is very attached to her mother, as many first graders are.

This little girl is charming, feminine, and needs a great deal of affection (numerous garlands and ringlets; majority of strokes are round). The many precise details of her drawing indicate a very observant, intelligent child who has great latent gifts for art. I predict that later on, when she becomes more independent, Mary will be happier.

playing   to   we are

playing   in   out

our   paddling   pool

Caroline Is 6

This is a rich, interesting sample. It tells me that Caroline is calm and obedient. I suspect that she tries to do well to please her teachers and her parents. Her writing reveals good concentration and reasoning ability. There is a great regularity in the size of the letters, the pressure and the baseline. She is healthy and well balanced but not particularly affectionate (round strokes are limited in her drawing). She prefers to read and write, and her manual abilities are not especially well developed.

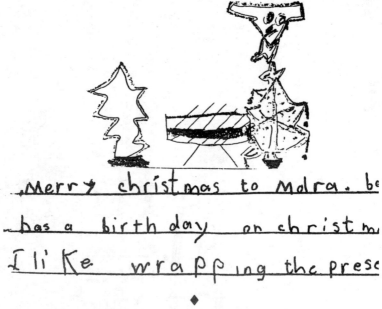

Merry christmas to Moira. be
has a birthday on christm
I like wrapping the prese

♦

Soon Moira Will Be 7

Her Christmas drawing is very lively, as Moira is. The colors (mostly shades of red and green) are bright and pleasant. The arms and the hands of the people in her picture are rather large. This reveals her inner aggressiveness. Her tree and her friend Caroline seem to be floating in the air. This placement, along with the light pressure, indicates that Moira has great imagination and sometimes fantasizes.

Her handwriting reveals that Moira's intelligence is advanced for her age (speedy, small, even size and light pressure; normal spacing). Emotionally, she appears young (meandering baseline). At school, she may be a handful. For example, she may be very witty and quick to learn but not yet willing to share with other children.

ne christmas caroline came to stayt
we pepd downsterd and wesaw mummy and
raping up presents we hatorun up sberd and t
bed wesurtid to irth and lrth andlrtn we redid
night wavg finshd and then we crepd dawn sterds
all arn presents we wackd up my mum my daddy and na
dressd and had arn breakfast in tow mints u
besd cows on and went tochurch when wecar

Josie Is 7

She is healthy and well balanced. Josie is a young 7-year-old who does not learn quickly. Her letters show various sizes and slants. Sexual emblems in her drawing reveal her continuing curiosity about sexuality. And note Moira's transparent dress. Josie feels a little lonely (exaggerated space between her words).

♦

Rohan Is 7

Her drawing is realistic. Rohan has practical abilities and good concentration. The campervan's wheels are planted solidly on the ground. It contains a bed, a table, and a stove. The large empty space above indicates that Rohan longs for freedom and independence, which is common at this age. Bright colors, yellow, blue, purple, red, and green, are applied with pressure, revealing her good health.

The strokes are sufficiently firm and straight to

assert that Rohan knows what she wants. She is pragmatic and well balanced. The predominantly round shapes of her letters reflect Rohan's feminity.

Rohan

This is a campervan 7

That we are going To Have when we go on Holiday

I went to the

I sor sum peple on a traplen and

Jessica Is 7½

Her numerous hearts and garlands and ringlets characterize a charming, healthy, and well-balanced girl. She
needs lots of affection. She is attached to her home.

The house is logically built, and everything is re-

Jessica
mond
wedD 7½

This is a PerSon
grdeD and he iS

PLaying in the
Doing theruting

lated to everything else. Jessica's printing is easy to read, with a regular baseline. All this means that her mind is organized and her concentration is good. The strong pressure and slow speed characterize health and physical maturity. Jessica is a realist. She enjoys playing sports. Her manual abilities are well developed. Intellectually, she is young.

◆

Felicity Is 8 Years Old

She prefers drawing and painting to writing. Felicity is very artistic. Her sense of proportion is well developed. She loves animals.

Her strokes are precise and firm and show a strong pressure. The girl is healthy, well-balanced, and lively. She is observant and perseverant. As long as she likes the activity, she will finish any task she starts and do it well.

◆

Katharine, 8 Years Old

She selected the colors brown, yellow, orange, purple, and green for her drawing. The dog's expression reveals Katharine's sense of humor as well as her affection for animals. She is observant and perseverant. Her power of concentration is advanced. She is healthy and well balanced. Her strokes combine the round, angular, and square, and in combination with the many details show that Katharine is sensitive, logical, and possesses technical and artistic gifts. I am sure that she is doing well at school.

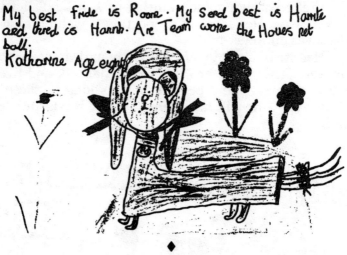

Following is another sample of Katharine's handwriting. We are going to analyze it together in detail. Until children have learned and are comfortable writing script, you may derive more from interpreting their artwork than their handwriting. Beginning here, and for many of the samples in the following chapters, I have prepared detailed handwriting analyses which are followed by Portraits of the writers. Once again you will see how children's personalities and abilities are revealed in their graphic expression.

8th November 1988. 500

Dea Rozane
Sorry that I did not come
late. I wolde have had a
ante come. I cant wate t
Stavday. Oh well must

from Katharine.

P.S.
You are my best
Friende

REMEMBER: In handwriting analysis, the interplay and accumulation of various signs together describe a specific character trait. In children, predominant and frequently recurring signs indicate either a predisposition toward or the actual development of a specific trait; that is, a trait more pronounced in the writer than in the majority of people in the corresponding age-group. Analyzing the details and the interplay of signs in many samples will help you to make the correct choice among several possible interpretations. In time, you will begin to form a general impression merely from glancing at a child's handwriting. However, your complete interpretation will always depend on the child's age-group and stage of development, and on your acknowledgment of the transitory nature of many aspects of character development during childhood.

Handwriting analysis

* Connected script: analytical and deductive mind.
* Slant goes backward and forward: normal at this age.
* Meandering baseline: restlessness.
* Strong, fairly regular pressure: good health; the child is well balanced.
* Letters are large and even in size: power of concentration, logical mind.
* Shape is mainly round: affectionate, feminine.
* Dots of the *i* high above its stem: imagination.
* Spacing is normal: well-balanced personality.
* A few overlapping strokes: she is perfecting her handwriting.
* End strokes are round, long, or absent: generosity or selfishness.

PORTRAIT OF KATHARINE: Her tenacity will enable her to meet her goals. She is able to concentrate and has the patience to finish whatever activity she starts. Her imagination and her sense of humor are good. She is well balanced and healthy. I suspect that she sulks when her parents refuse to satisfy her wishes, but rarely is she moody or temperamental.

At this age, the meandering baseline and the variable slant reflect emotional and social maturation. For example, at rare moments, Katharine may hesitate and not know how to behave in front of grown-ups or strangers. She appears slightly timid and unsure of herself, a common phenomenon and quite normal in her age-group. Likewise, at times she may be very generous and at other moments rather selfish.

◆

Nelly Is 9 Years Old

Her drawing of two small lions ornaments Nelly's note. The pressure is strong; this means the child is healthy. The general aspect suggests to me that Nelly has a happy disposition.

Handwriting analysis:

- Large and round: affectionate, feminine child.
- Straight baseline: well-balanced disposition.
- Slight backward slant: common at this age.
- Knotted loops (see *f*): great tenacity, perseverance; stubbornness.

NELLY'S PORTRAIT: If you look at her writing for a while, you can feel the effort of Nelly's pen to fight the backward slant and get it straightened up. I suspect that she is outgrowing the natural timidity of the small child. She is trying to be more spontaneous and to assert her charming, feminine, affectionate nature. Emotionally, Nelly is well balanced but can be stubborn. Eager to obey, once she grabs on to a project, she perseveres until it's complete.

5

The Older Child
9 to 12

As children mature, their timidity and anxiety diminish. Their personalities develop along individual paths. They grapple with the physical, intellectual, social, and emotional changes that mark this period of growth.

For example, at 10 or 11, children are less egocentric than before and less attached to their mothers. Often their need for open affection diminishes during this period. Social integration slowly sets in. Children in this age-group love to scare one another and adults. They play hide and seek, put creepy rubber animals in their parents' beds, and cover themselves with fake blood to pretend they are wounded, among other acts of mischief. If they succeed in scaring their friends or their parents, they can burst into laughter until their faces are covered with tears. They might become boisterous and completely unafraid. They love sports and may be inclined to roughhousing. Often, they prefer commercials to anything else on TV.

Their developing sense of responsibility heightens during this period. When they have a bad day at school or lose in some sports competition, they are less likely to blame their parents or "the world." Instead, they take the blame on themselves, for being lazy, stupid, or incompetent. In fact, some children work too hard at school at this age. They become exhausted physically and mentally. You might notice it in their writing, which will show a baseline plunging downward, irregular pressure, and imprecise letters, which are difficult to read.

Children's handwriting and drawings show how they are changing and what they're going through. Each child is individual, so remember to remain flexible. The meaning of specific strokes will vary from one sample to another. The exact nuance depends in each case on the general aspect of the sample you are analyzing. You must take into account the interaction of all the strokes. For instance, the significance of any slant is not the same in a slow hand as in a speedy one. Your ability to interpret children's graphics will improve as you continue to evaluate more and more samples. Eventually, you will be able to grasp the main traits of an unknown child simply by analyzing the general aspect of a writing sample or drawing. The trick is keeping in mind constantly that each child is an individual who is growing and changing. The range of behavior that we may consider as normal within each age-group is wide.

Between 9 and 12, children start making plans for the future. They are all anxious to grow up fast and be independent. The freedom of adults seems magical to them. We can see this urge to escape and be free in their drawings and handwriting, which becomes more progressive, showing a rightward slant.

Some children reach puberty by the age of 12 or

even before. Physical changes can appear quickly and cause some anxiety, which most kids try to hide. They become very sensitive toward any remarks or criticism from their friends. They can be bashful and self-conscious of their bodies or exaggeratedly proud of being early bloomers. Often their attitudes are extreme: either they choose to shut sexuality completely out of their lives or they show too much interest in it and begin to neglect their schoolwork and other interests.

Watch out for emerging inhibitions during these years. Remember that interpretations of drawings and handwriting of children in this age-group must remain flexible. Discuss your discoveries openly with your child and emphasize that you are there to help. Kids appreciate honesty and efforts to understand them better. Even though children at this age seem to be pulling away a bit, their personalities are still malleable, and you can influence them for the better as they approach their teen years.

Samples

Ebony Is 9 Years Old

The combined effect of her drawings and her short, spontaneous poem leads me to believe that Ebony is artistically gifted. The somehow monotonous aspect of her willow tree is balanced by her quick, light handwriting. Ebony is rather sensitive and remains timid. Her health may be fragile, but her outlook on life is energetic and optimistic.

NOTE: Some psychologists contend that trees with downward-reaching branches signal depression. Graphologists do not agree with this hypothesis.

A Pet to own

I could choose a dog to own,
But in Kennels there all alone.

I could choose a cat, ~~~~
That would live it's life in my straw
hat.
I could choose a Frog,

ut I would miss it on it's daily Jog.

I could choose a bear,
oh no! It would grab my chair.

I could choose a pig,
Noooo, he would mess up my house
with is silly Jig's.

Handwriting analysis:

- Clear and easy to read: organized, logical, respects other people.
- Light, regular pressure: intelligence, vivacity, quick mind; fear; timidity; fragility.
- Fairly straight baseline: organized, well-balanced child who obeys parents and teachers.
- Speedy, disconnected script: intuition, intellect.
- Regular, slightly progressive slant: curiosity; optimism; dynamism.
- Round shape: affectionate, feminine.
- Some altered letters: possible anxiety or insecurity.

PORTRAIT OF EBONY: Ebony is charming, affectionate, and sensitive and appears to be in the midst of some inner struggles for greater independence. I suspect that if a grown-up scowls at her, she may feel hurt and burst into tears. She's restless and feels insecure, as do many in her age-group.

Ebony is very intelligent, intuitive, and quick. She is organized and has an excellent memory. Her poem reveals her intellectual creativity.

During adolescence Ebony will be challenged to overcome her sensitivity and her inhibitions. As her parent, I would be on the lookout for potential eating problems.

◆

Mary-Anne Is 9 Years Old

Here we see her drawing and a small sample of her handwriting. Mary-Anne's strokes are strong and precise. The colors (yellow, green, red, and brown) are bright and complement one another. Her concentration is strong. She is organized, and she knows what she wants. She is very independent. Mary-Anne is obviously healthy, well balanced, and happy. Even without considering her handwriting, we can come to these conclusions.

Dear Miranda,

having me,
the weather.

Thankyou so much for
We were really lucky on

Lots of Love

Handwriting analysis:

- Regular and easy to read: well-balanced child; respect for other people.
- Fairly straight baseline; well-balanced, organized.
- Round shape: femininity; need for affection and gratification.
- Slow speed: writer does not follow her impulses blindly, but thinks and reasons first; she knows how to concentrate.
- *t* crossing is short, strong, in the middle: strong willpower.
- Strong pressure: good health, robust person.

- Dots on the *i* are very high: imagination.
- End strokes of the letters are long: generosity.
- Lower loops of letters *y* and *g* open and pointing backward: sexual inhibition or ambivalence.
- Upright script: well-balanced, sensible person; lack of spontaneity.
- Wide spacing between words and lines: writer is not very sociable; great need for independence and freedom.

MARY-ANNE'S PORTRAIT: Mary-Anne is mature for her 9 years. In fact, she will soon be 10. She has a strong, independent personality and probably longs for the freedom older children enjoy. She is a healthy girl, and it is evident in her handwriting that she is experiencing the first hints of sexual awakening; this is not uncommon among 9-to-12 year olds.

I assume that Mary-Anne's willpower, imagination, and ability to concentrate help her in her studies. She appears cooperative and obedient to adults in authority. She is even-tempered, sensible, organized, punctual, and something of a loner. She is neither impulsive nor spontaneous, and I suspect that at times she feels a little lonely.

◆

Rosi Is 10 Years Old

Around this age children often refuse to draw, especially if you ask them. As they become more independent,

they often become more stubborn. Rosi's drawing is small but well proportioned. It represents a happy little girl like her.

Dear suzy
right now I in paris I haver much fun here How are you I'm f I hope you're enjoying you're (you two weeks holidays) where write back to me and tel what youre doing

Rosi

Handwriting analysis:

- Variable shape, size, slant: instability; insecurity; restlessness.
- Medium, regular pressure: good physical health.
- Altered and overlapping strokes: dissemblance; shyness; fear, anxiety.
- Ringlets and coils: selfishness; seductiveness.
- High *i* dots: imagination.
- Meandering baseline: common at this age; moody or temperamental.
- Irregular spacing: need for independence; loneliness.
- Connected script: logical.
- Variable lower loops: inhibitions; awakening of sexuality.

ROSI'S PORTRAIT: Rosi is in good physical health, vivacious, and imaginative. She often invents stories and confabulates. Her parents never know quite whether she is telling the truth: she has the ability to dissemble, or conceal information. She is capable of being charming and seductive in order to get what she wants. Rosi is extremely lively and needs to move a lot. She has no patience. She is a "young" 10 year old.

Rosi would like to be more independent but cannot assume responsibility. Her parents watch her almost constantly, so that she doesn't get into mischief. Often she is boisterous and refuses to obey. She can be stubborn, irrational, and very selfish. Rosi has feelings of inferiority, which produce anxiety and anguish. She is nervous, restless, and insecure. I suspect that she's not a good eater and that her moodiness and temper are affecting her schoolwork.

◆

Helen Is 11

Her drawing is precise. The lion shows his teeth; this means he is dangerous.

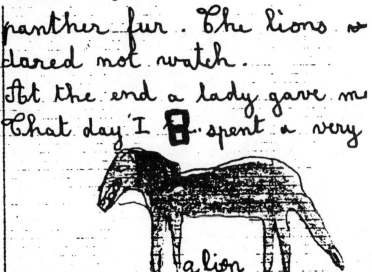

Handwriting analysis:

- Clear, easy to read: well-balanced, obedient child who respects other people.
- Strong, regular pressure: good health.
- Medium, regular size: logical, well-balanced thinking; maturity.
- Upright slant: sensible; not impulsive; strong concentration.
- Knotted loops (see *t* and *s*: perseverance, tenacity, stubbornness.
- Coils: selfishness; materialistic tendencies.
- The *t* crossing is in the upper part of the stem, which shows an overlapping stroke: strong willpower; ability to hide feelings.
- Connected script: analytical and deductive mind; lack of intuition.

HELEN'S PORTRAIT: She is intelligent and mature for her age. Her manual and intellectual abilities are excellent. Helen is healthy, well-balanced, and capable of assuming some responsibility, for she is extremely sensible. She is logical but her intuition is limited. Her disposition is even, and there is an inhibited aspect evident in her script.

Although Helen is attached to her parents and friends, she is not very sociable. She lacks spontaneity: her attitude is critical, and she thinks before she acts.

Helen has a good visual memory, strong powers of concentration, and is very realistic. Her willpower is strong.

There is an aspect of selfishness and aggressiveness in Helen's script. I suspect that at times she can be generous, but not very often; it's usually "me first."

♦

Emma Is 11 Years Old

She refuses to draw, but this small sample of her writing gives us some clues to her personality.

sweets and pretty animals are Rabbits cats yours? I love

things my favorite horses and dogs what are

Handwriting analysis:

- Regular, medium pressure: good health.
- Meandering baseline: normal.
- Small to medium size: intelligence, maturity.
- Fast speed: intelligence, intellectual creativity; vivacious spirit.
- Variable slant: emotional instability.
- Connected script: logic and memory.
- High *i* dots: imagination and creativity.
- Regular spacing: well-balanced person.
- Knotted loops: perseverance; powers of concentration.
- Some overlapping strokes: diplomacy; dissemblance.
- Round shape: need for affection; femininity.

EMMA'S PORTRAIT: Even though we have only a small sample to analyze, by this point in your study you should be able to identify the general aspect of Emma's handwriting and to speculate on her overall personality.

The variable slant and meandering baseline clue us in to the changeable feelings and range of emotions that confront the typical 11 year old, who is on the verge of adolescence yet firmly entrenched in childhood. The remaining features of Emma's script reveal that she is coping nicely with the normal conflicts of growing up. She is sociable, sensible, and sensitive. Despite her inner impatience, her strong concentration and tenacity enable her to handle responsibility.

I suspect that her parents are pleased with Emma and that everyone admires her wit and intelligence. She is mature for her age, in good health, and very intelligent.

◆

Betty, Age 11

Claude,

Today we celebrated

He got alot of nice

ous for my friend s

Handwriting analysis:

- Very large and round: need for affection and attention; childishness; femininity.
- Medium to weak pressure: psychologically fragile; sensitive.
- Overlapping strokes: anxiety; dissemblance; lack of spontaneity; insecurity.
- Ringlets: seductiveness; manipulative behavior.
- Coils: selfishness.
- Some knotted loops: perseverance or stubbornness.
- Slightly variable slant: normal; ambivalence.
- Clear and easy to read: respect for other people.

BETTY'S PORTRAIT: Unlike Emma, Betty is a young 11. She is charming and feminine but basically insecure. She needs lots of affection and attention. Betty is good at hiding her feelings and inhibitions. She may be developing an inferiority complex.

She can be insincere and selfish. At school she may show off or perform to get attention. She has both artistic and theatrical talents, and she needs movement. Perhaps she is a dancer.

As Betty matures, her constant need for attention and her ambivalent emotions should subside, but I suspect that to a degree these characteristics will always be a part of her personality.

◆

Regina, Age 12

Her artistic talent and strong concentration are obvious. The strokes are firm and confident. Regina is healthy and talented. Her writing sample reveals additional facets of her personality.

The manager has either ti
friends.
When was the name of t
changed?
The Brown's family don'
Mary's children anymore
Jimmy has fallen into the
George often waters.

Handwriting analysis:

- Regular but not monotonous: logic, order, rational thinking.
- Medium to large size: childlike qualities.
- Round shape: affectionate; feminine.
- Pronounced arcades: ability to manipulate others; inner arrogance.
- Medium, regular pressure: well-balanced, healthy child.
- Speedy: quick mind; vivacity; intelligence.
- Connected and disconnected script: mature; intuitive; intellectual; artistic.
- Exaggerated middle zone: realistic; materialistic.
- Rather tight spacing: selfish; economical; attached to parents and friends.
- Backward slant: physical inhibitions; dissemblance; egocentric behavior—all normal during adolescence.
- Ringlets: seductive; manipulative.
- End strokes absent: selfishness.
- Regular, firm *t* crossings: strong willpower.
- Clear and readable writing: respect for other people; politeness.
- Straight baseline: well-balanced; sensible; logical.

PORTRAIT OF REGINA: At school, Regina is working at two years above her grade-level. She appears emotionally and physically mature as well. She's a realist with a strong, positive self-image. She's ambitious and likes to win. In fact, I think that she expects to win and feels that she deserves to win. She wants to become a lawyer.

At 12, Regina is very much an adolescent, clinging just a bit to childhood.

♦

Mark Is 12

Here's a concise interpretation—a sketch rather than a portrait—that represents the sort of information you will begin to glean from absorbing the overall aspect of a sample rather than from analyzing each stroke in detail.

While Mark's drawing appears to be the work of a younger child, his handwriting contradicts this first impression of immaturity. His script (fast, medium pressure, straight baseline) reveals that Mark is intelligent, imaginative, healthy, and well balanced. The slight backward slant and a few altered strokes signal his approaching adolescence—and the attendant insecurity that often accompanies puberty.

Mark is restless, possibly a consequence of his awakening sexuality, and he may appear vain (high stems) in an attempt to compensate for his feelings of

insecurity or inferiority. Finally, Mark's signature (embellished script) reinforces first the notion of vanity and second the immaturity we saw in his drawings. This sample provides an excellent snapshot of the child maturing into a teenager.

Dear Claude,

Welcome to (

I quite like it here, the good and at the moment playing Rugby. My best sp. Athletics. I like English a lot a very good subject and we do interesting things

from

Mark

6

The Young Adolescent 12 to 15

If a child hasn't refused to draw by now, look for it to happen. Perhaps it's stubbornness, independence, fear of criticism, or lack of interest. As they undergo rapid mental and physical changes, young teenagers' handwriting might temporarily deteriorate. How much should you worry?

First remember that aggressiveness, stubbornness, and obstinacy are normal in the young teen. Whatever activity or behavior you propose or even remotely suggest to your teenager will be refused vigorously. Teenagers want to follow their own heads and to obtain freedom of action and thought. They do not feel like children anymore, yet they know they are not quite adults. Some run away from home. Even with all the bad press they get, the overwhelming majority of adolescents overcome the trials of puberty successfully.

If you have a good relationship with your teenager,

you will continue to face minor dramas daily. Your child may refuse to wash or change clothes. I knew a little boy who loved to swim. When he was 13, his mother was beside herself trying to figure out how to get him to wash. Her strategy was to take him to the swimming pool in order to get him into the water. But her son figured it out and told her, "Since your idea is to get me clean, I'll never swim again!"

Another youngster had studied well at school up to this age. Suddenly she refused to concentrate, do her homework, or obey teachers. In both cases, the youngsters may have been affected by their emerging sex drive, their attempts to be independent, and/or an inability to communicate their feelings.

Beware the signs of eating disorders in girls of this age-group (one is numerous tapered strokes). Such self-destructive behavior can be a girl's reaction to feelings of depression or a passive way of expressing violent feelings of aggression.

Other teenagers develop cyclothymic tendencies—mood swings to you and me—that appear for no apparent reason. They can burst into prolonged laughter which may bring them to tears. At other times they cry or sulk for hours on end. Moodiness certainly lies within the normal range of behavior during this period of rapid growth and maturation. For the most part, it's temporary. Rare are parents who never have any difficulties with their young teenager.

Young adolescents may become very competitive in all areas. They like to measure their physical strength against friends or family, for instance. (And sometimes they don't know their own strength!) Their emotions are frequently contradictory—in one situation, perhaps, too aggressive and in another too timid.

The complex combination of intellectual and physical maturation can add to adolescents' general frustrations. More or less consciously, they rebel. It is difficult for their parents to understand them. For example, an honest, easy-going child might suddenly start lying or stealing, only to attract attention. Sexual acting-out is common.

Young adolescents are usually extremely sensitive and vulnerable. They may develop feelings of inferiority. You can detect interior conflicts in their drawings and handwriting: the pressure becomes spasmodic and irregular; the slant goes backward toward the left; the letters are altered or difficult to read; many coils appear. If the baseline suddenly drops downward, psychological conflicts are beginning to affect your teen's physical health.

You have to study many handwritten samples in order to progress in analyzing teenagers. The general instability you may see in their graphics is only temporary, so be especially tolerant in your interpretations. Keep in mind that the meaning of any stroke can vary. For instance, generally speaking small script depicts intelligence, masculinity, and maturity. However, if the baseline meanders and the pressure is light, scratch the maturity aspect. If the shape is round, scratch masculinity. By continuing to evaluate many samples, your abilities will improve, and your choices will be correct.

Samples

Leigh Is 12

*. How are you today ?
cticut. I am twelve years
is coming up soon on
dog, a cat, a bird and
like to play the cello, french-
ride my bicycle. I have
'nie that I've known
r over to her house alot
tell, I've got to go now.*

Handwriting analysis:

- Strong pressure: good health.
- Medium size, regular spacing: logical, well-balanced thinking.
- Easy to read: polite; clear concentration.
- Regular and strong *t* crossings: willpower.
- Slightly progressive slant: aggressive, ambitious; spontaneous; hard worker.

- Regular, straight baseline: even disposition.
- Shape, round and angular: mature; dynamic; logical.
- Long, upward end strokes: generosity.
- Upper, middle, and lower zone similar in size: mature; well rounded.
- Some tapered end strokes: destructive tendencies.
- Long, lifting initial strokes of words: critical mind; sense of humor.
- Some overlapping strokes: diplomacy; dissemblance; discretion.
- Connected script: analytical and deductive mind; sociability; attachment to parents and friends.
- High *i* dots: imagination.
- Some coils and hooks: selfishness; onset of puberty.
- Medium speed: sensible; not impulsive.
- Regular, full, and finished lower loops: need for affection; normal libido; need for physical movement; sports.

LEIGH'S PORTRAIT: This girl is very healthy and well-balanced. Leigh is intelligent, and she knows what she wants. Her concentration and her willpower are strong. She is perseverant. She can be stubborn.

She is sociable, dynamic, and spontaneous, but knows how to be discreet or diplomatic if it's called for. She has an even disposition.

Leigh is athletic, imaginative, artistic. She's a mature 12—ready to enjoy her teen years.

♦

Griffin Is a Boy of 12

Note that this sample was written with a felt-tip pen. As you read my handwriting analysis, take a close look at the general aspect of the handwriting. Try to get a feel for the interaction of all the strokes. The interdependence of these factors affects the interpretation of each

128

stroke and accounts for the varying meanings that might be assigned to a given characteristic. For instance, the meaning of a slant is not quite the same in a slow, monotonous writing as it is in a fast, lively script.

Thank you so for the money. It m kind of you to give to me. I am going get a tennis racket yours and other people's that they gave me I have recently bec interested in learning play.

Hope to see you perhaps Dad can

Handwriting analysis:

- Round shape: need for affection and gratification; ambivalence; charm.
- Rather slow speed: latent artistic talent; lack of spontaneity; slow reasoning; immaturity.
- Wide spacing: need for independence; loneliness.
- Pronounced middle zone: materialistic and realistic person.
- Straight baseline: healthy and well-balanced person.

- Strong pressure: good physical health.
- Open lower loops: unsatisfactory fulfillment of the libido; normal in this age-group.
- Clear, readable, connected script: sociability, politeness, attachment to parents and friends.
- Straight or slight backward slant: logical thinking; slight physical inhibition and awakening of sexuality; stubbornness.
- End strokes are absent: selfishness.

GRIFFIN'S PORTRAIT: Poised at puberty, Griffin is well balanced and very healthy, but intellectually rather slow and emotionally immature. Basically, he is extremely selfish and insensitive. He can be stubborn and cowardly. His first love may be sports or some other manual activity.

Typical of his age-group, Griffin has a great need for affection and gratification. He's charming and, I suspect, still very attached to his mother. I detect some sexual ambivalence, not at all unusual at this stage of development.

♦

Paul Is 12

The angular strokes in his drawing show that Paul is clever and virile. He is sociable and has a good sense of humor (facial expression).

Dear Claude,

I hope you are having a nice France. I wish to see you abouts in France do you in Hickling, and I am from

Paul Talk

Handwriting analysis:

- Medium size: intelligent and balanced.
- Angular shape: quick, clever mind; passion for intellectual activity; curious; dynamic; virile; ambitious; selfish; cruel or tough.
- Medium pressure: good health; well-balanced child.
- Speedy: quick understanding; vivacious; intelligent; irritable.
- Wide spacing: need for independence; slight intellectual loneliness.
- Progressive slant, slightly variable at times: dynamic, ambitious; passionate; spontaneous; restless.
- Meandering baseline: excitability; irritability; restlessness.
- Clear, readable, connected script: sociability; politeness; attachment to parents and friends.
- Slightly inhibited script: selfishness; meanness; avaricious tendencies.

PAUL'S PORTRAIT: Paul, like Leigh, is mature for his age. His goals are high. He expects a lot from himself and from other people. He is intelligent, sociable, and spontaneous, but at times is rather irritable and self-ish. His personality is independent and virile. Paul's need for affection is limited, although he is attached to his parents. His physical health is good. Some inner instability and anxiety appear at times. When a chosen activity pleases Paul, he can show a great passion for it and finish it brilliantly, and this is normal.

Intellectually he sometimes feels slightly lonely. His dynamic personality and strong willpower will enable him to succeed in life. However, problems might occur in his private life; he must learn the art of compromise, modify his high expectations of those around him, and control his selfish, tough, or mean impulses.

♦

Andrew Is 13

Andrew is a healthy, well-balanced adolescent. He is slightly ambivalent regarding his sexuality, which is normal during adolescence. His drawings show some round strokes and some ringlets; revealing Andrew's sociability and compliance. The face of the man has a beard—Andrew would like to be grown up—at the same time the idea scares him—the open mouth shows a big tooth.

d same

saccn. Today in am going in a game of Rugby. I am probably going to play game of Squash. Would you to come and visit me.

bay

Andrew wilde bay

A.S.W

Handwriting analysis:

- Strong, regular pressure: good health; well-balanced child.
- Round and angular shape: well-balanced and mature.
- Medium size and speed: maturity.
- Lower loops open and pointing backward: sexual awakening and ambivalence; the person is sexually unsatisfied.
- Backward slant: inhibition, egocentric behavior, selfishness, lack of spontaneity and honesty—normal transient phenomena in this age-group.
- Wide spacing: need for independence; loneliness.
- Straight baseline: well-balanced and responsible.
- Clear, easy-to-read, connected script: sociably polite person.
- Ringlets: sociability; manipulative behavior; seductiveness.

ANDREW'S PORTRAIT: In the throes of adolescence, Andrew's composure is exceptional. He is obedient and well behaved but increasingly aware of his sexuality. The ambivalence evident in his script is temporary.

Andrew would like to be older and be free to do what he wants. He has strong concentration and an excellent memory. A profession where he is surrounded by other people would suit his extremely sociable nature. Perhaps Andrew will become a diplomat, a lawyer, or a public relations expert.

◆

Maxine Is 13

Maxine is the only child of older parents. Her drawing depicts an African girl. Her strokes are mainly round. Look at the ringlets. Maxine is feminine and charming,

Dear claude.

I thought I'd send you England is very humid at the n most of the time. At this mome cup of hot - chocolate to satisj about my, Claude, tell me u I'm very interested in knowing eat at the moment?

yours s

healthy, happy, and well balanced. She dreams of exotic adventures and freedom. Her manual dexterity is well developed.

Handwriting analysis:

- Medium size: well-balanced child.
- Round shape: affectionate and feminine.
- Straight slant: sensible, reasonable, well-balanced person; excellent concentration.
- Fairly straight baseline: even disposition.
- Strong pressure: good physical health; manual abilities.
- Strong, even *t* crossings: strong willpower.
- Ringlets: Sociable; seductive or manipulative.
- Open lower loops: awakening of the libido; dreams of love.
- Inhibited aspect—spacing is normal between lines and words but tight between letters: well-balanced, but selfish.
- Some tapered strokes: destructive or aggressive tendencies.
- Pronounced middle zone: materialistic and realistic.
- Some overlapping strokes and altered letters: anxiety.
- Clear, connected script: sociable; polite; attached to family and friends.

PORTRAIT OF MAXINE: Maxine, whose parents always have indulged her, says that she hopes to marry a wealthy businessman and have many children. I imagine that she is adept at using her feminine charm in seductive and manipulative ways. She is cunning, and she lives in the present: her strong willpower and concentration make her a real go-getter, and what she wants is immediate, material gratification.

Maxine is intelligent, organized, and responsible. She's artistic, and her talents appear to extend from drawing and painting to dancing and acting. But because Maxine is so focused on the present, she is not especially eager to plan for faraway goals. She's certainly capable of going on to college, but she might not acquire the patience to complete her studies there.

♦

Miranda Is 13

Dear Claude,

I am 13 years old. My ... in Larchmont, New York; but English. Here, I live in Edinbr I am in set three in Fre average.

How does the print look better than the script?

Signed,
Miranda M.

Handwriting analysis:

- Variable pressure, slant, and shape: emotional instability; precarious health; restlessness.
- Meandering baseline: inhibited; moody.

- Connected script: sociable and polite; attached to parents and friends.
- Speedy: intelligence; quick mind; vivacious spirit.
- Tapering end strokes: destructive or aggressive tendencies.
- Knotted loops: perseverance, tenacity.
- Overlapping strokes: dissemblance.
- Coils: selfishness; need for material gratification.
- Round initial strokes: sense of humor; critical mind; intelligence.
- Difficult to read: lacks respect for others; selfishness.

MIRANDA'S PORTRAIT: She is highly intelligent and mature for her age. Her mind is quick and sharp. She has a good sense of humor and a vivacious spirit. But Miranda also is rather impatient, irritable, and restless. In fact, she is so active that I imagine she has trouble concentrating and controlling her behavior.

She is capable of concealing her feelings and thoughts, and her parents may have trouble knowing when she's lying and when she's telling the truth. Miranda is selfish, and she can treat her family and friends badly.

The onset of adolescence has thrown Miranda for a loop. I suspect that her behavior may range from overactive to completely inactive, her emotions may be completely unstable, and her health fragile. Miranda requires a physical outlet, such as sports or dance.

◆

Annie Is 13

Dear Dick,

    I hope you are well because I am. I have got a hockey lesson soon so I had better go now.

Lots of love
ANNIE
13 years (GIRL).

Handwriting analysis:

- Strong pressure: good physical health.
- Straight baseline: well-balanced child; even disposition.
- Slightly backward slant: Normal at this age; selfishness; power of concentration; physical inhibitions; lack of spontaneity.
- Clear, slightly embellished script (see capital letters): childlike behavior; lack of intelligence; respect for other people.
- Slightly inhibited script: inhibitions; selfishness.
- Pronounced middle zone: need for affection and gratification; materialistic tendencies.

- Slow speed: slow thinking; laziness; manual ability.
- Disconnected script: intuitive and independent; in a slow script, can mean a lack of intelligence.
- Very round shape: affectionate and feminine.
- Round, large, open lower loops: awakening of sexuality; unsatisfied libido; need for affection.

ANNIE'S PORTRAIT: Typical of children during the teen years, Annie refuses to draw. I suspect that she likes sports, games, and social events but doesn't care much for school or intellectual pursuits.

Annie is a "young" 13. She's egocentric, happy-go-lucky, and independent. Doing well at school isn't important to her, nor are college or a career. I imagine that she's interested in having a good time and attached to material things. Annie is respectful, obedient, affectionate, and a little lazy.

◆

Samuel Is 13

His drawing is stylized and extremely simplified. Samuel is sensible, logical, and mature. The square, straight lines reveal his technical abilities. The angular strokes depict his virility.

Dear Claude,

Hello. I really enjoy this and what happens here. I quite the English lessons, and I don't fall to sleep during them. Most of time, too I am doing rides from members of staff, and my name u becomes extremely annoyed with u

Samuel G G

Samuel G. Gough.

Age: 13 Boy

Handwriting analysis:

- Small size: quick mind; maturity; virility; intelligence.
- Round and angular shapes: maturity; intellectual ability.
- Speedy: vivaciousness; impatience and irritability; intelligence.
- Medium, regular pressure: intellectual creativity; good health.
- Normal, regular spacing: logical, well-balanced child.
- Backward slant: inhibition; sexual awakening; diplomacy or dissemblance; egocentric tendencies; selfishness.
- Lower loops open and sinistrogyric: sexual ambivalence and lack of satisfaction; normal for this age-group.
- Altered letters: irritability; anxiety; dissemblance.
- Some knotted lower loops: perserverance; sexual problems.

- Straight, descending baseline: organized, well-balanced child, who is sometimes slightly depressed or discouraged.
- Connected script: analytical and deductive mind; sociable; attached to friends and parents.

SAMUEL'S PORTRAIT: Intellectually, Samuel is advanced. His mind is quick, analytical, and deductive. He plans to go on to college, and with the correct guidance and application, Samuel will succeed in any career he chooses, from medicine to journalism to engineering (even though he is not manually inclined).

Although he is healthy and well balanced, Samuel is confronting his awakening sexuality, which sometimes causes him confusion. As a result, he may feel depressed or discouraged at times. All these circumstances are normal at puberty, and I predict that Samuel will grow into a well-adjusted teenager.

◆

Lucy Is 13

Her drawing is small and very round; apparently, she has a great need for affection.

r Claude,

I have just come think it is good
port , netball , hocke
ry. The weather to
s , but warm, and
might rain later.
Lucy croton.

Handwriting analysis:

- Strong, regular pressure: healthy, well-balanced child.
- Medium, regular size: well-balanced.
- Very round shape: feminine and affectionate child.
- Slow speed: laziness; lack of intelligence.
- Straight baseline: even temperament.
- Tapering end strokes: selfishness; destructive tendencies.
- Straight slant with some sinistrogyric strokes: normal at this age; ability to concentrate; selfishness; egocentric tendencies.
- Overlapping strokes: dissemblance.
- Coils: selfish; materialistic.
- Pronounced middle zone: need for immediate gratification; materialistic; realistic.
- *i* dot in a circle (embellished letter): childlike behavior; dissemblance; selfishness.

- Open lower loops: lack of sexual satisfaction; reduced libido; normal phenomenon in this age-group.
- Arcades: compliance.
- Clear, connected script: sociability, respect for others.

LUCY'S PORTRAIT: Lucy is an even tempered, compliant child who is very feminine and sociable. It's likely that she's highly susceptible to peer pressure and anxious to go along with the crowd. I suspect that her parents always have indulged her, for there are plentiful signs of selfishness, materialism, and laziness in her script.

Emotionally, Lucy is young for her age. She appears to demand immediate gratification of her wants, and she is capable of lying if need be to get what she thinks she needs. Lucy is not particularly ambitious or talented.

◆

Mark Is 14

His drawings show his technical ability and his virility.

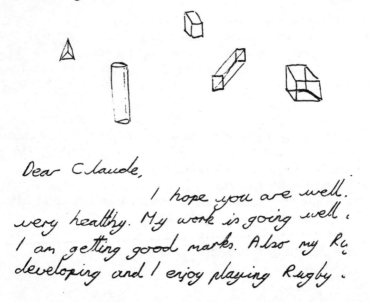

Dear Claude,
              I hope you are well.
very healthy. My work is going well.
I am getting good marks. Also my Ru
developing and I enjoy playing Rugby.

Handwriting analysis:

- Progressive slant: dynamic; ambitious; spontaneous.
- Medium to small size: logical; virile.
- Clear, connected script: sociable and polite; attached to parents and friends.
- Medium to fast speed: the boy is lively but impulsive.
- End strokes mostly visible: generosity.
- Reduced spacing, especially between letters: economical or thrifty.
- Open lower loops: unsettled libido; unfulfilled dreams of physical love; sexual ambivalence.
- Some sticklike stems in the letters: idealism; could turn fanatical and cruel.
- Descending baseline: illness; sadness; depression.
- Slightly monotonous script: possible regression; neurotic tendencies.
- Fairly round shape, except the sticklike strokes: need for affection.

MARK'S PORTRAIT: Mark is in the midst of his own adolescent sexual ambivalence, which is typical of his age-group. These normal and transient inhibitions combine with several inherent contradictory tendencies, such as his natural spontaneity or his generous yet economical nature. I think that Mark is feeling the weight of growing up and yearns to return to childhood, which is comfortable, familiar, and safe.

With the love and support of his family, Mark will make it through this transition to adulthood just fine. He is ambitious, intelligent, and virile.

◆

Malke Is a Boy of 14

Dear Claude,

This morning I

lessons one of my

where we were looked a

writing which the lady

us and she was g

From

Matke

Handwriting analysis:

- Strong, regular pressure: good health.
- Round shape: affectionate and feminine.
- Pronounced middle zone: realism; materialism.
- Large size: immaturity; feminine charm; vanity; artistic talent.
- Slow speed: slow reasoning and thinking; manual abilities.
- Overlapping strokes: dissemblance; hypocrisy; inhibition; anxiety.
- Variable slant: emotional instability.
- End strokes are absent: selfishness.
- Variable spacing: instability.
- Variable full and wavy lower loops: homosexual tendencies.
- Ringlets: feminine charm; sociability; seductive and manipulative behavior.

- Altered letters: anxiety.
- Twisted strokes in the upper zone: glandular or other temporary health problems, not uncommon in this age-group.
- Script which is difficult to read: little respect for others; dissemblance; anxiety.
- Pronounced arcades: arrogance; selfishness.
- Absence of initial strokes; immature; gullible.
- Straight baseline: even disposition.

MALKE'S PORTRAIT: Unlike most adolescents, Malke's sexuality is not ambivalent: he is admittedly homosexual. Malke is very charming and sociable. He knows how to manipulate people and situations in order to get what he wants. His manner is effeminate.

He is in good physical health and has an even temperament, but sometimes he gets anxious because his emotions are, in typical adolescent fashion, unstable. Malke knows how to conceal his feelings. He is very artistic but not very intellectually inclined.

◆

Rory, a Boy of 15

Dear Claude.
This morning I have had five
which were really horrible.
were English, Maths, Geogra
French, and now it's English
again.

R.P.C.

Rory Long.

aged 15

male.

Handwriting analysis:

- Strong, regular pressure: good health; stable personality.
- Variable size (medium and small): intelligence; virility; emotional instability.
- Round and angular shape: maturity.
- Absent or very high *i* dots: lack of concentration; good imagination.
- End strokes absent or tapered and launching upward: selfish; active temper; destructive tendencies.
- Superfluous dots at ends of lines: lack of trust in other people; he mistrusts everyone and is able to lie when it is useful.
- Connected script: analytical and deductive mind.
- Variable slant: inhibitions; emotional instability.
- Closed and full lower loops: heterosexual libido.
- Very meandering baseline: instability; irritability; poor concentration.
- Altered letters: anxiety.
- Fast speed: vivacity; intelligence, wit.
- Space normal to wide between words: need for independence; inner loneliness.

RORY'S PORTRAIT: Here again we see some contradictory personality traits. Rory is unsettled. He craves variety in all areas of his life in order to satisfy his intellectual talents and moodiness. He's highly intelligent and intolerant of those who don't grasp concepts as quickly as he does. I suspect that he can be rather difficult and willful.

He is lazy and has limited concentration, perhaps because he's never had to work very hard to master any task. He lacks trust and confidence in others and appears untrustworthy himself.

♦

Anthony, Age 15

Dear Claude,

Here I am, sitting in a t
lemon. Not exactly the most ea
thing around. As you may have n
Thursday today, my worst day
I should be playing games
exactly play because I'm
way I better go. yours sincerely.

Handwriting analysis:

- Medium to light pressure: poor health; wit; intelligence.
- Extremely progressive slant: dynamic, spontaneous, and passionate; ambitious.
- Size (small in the middle zone; high stems; long, closed loops): virility; idealism; healthy sexuality.
- Speedy: intelligence, wit.
- High *i* dots: good imagination.
- Ascendent baseline: optimistic disposition.
- Altered letters: slight anxiety or timidity.
- Wide spacing: independent or a little lonely.
- Slightly jumbled script (loops falling into the following line): mental confusion; in this case, need for a physical outlet.
- Connected script: sociable; attached to parents and friends.

ANTHONY'S PORTRAIT: Anthony has recurring bouts with asthma. He needs to watch what he eats and get plenty of sleep. In spite of this, he is physically active and good at sports. His youthful enthusiasm and passionate nature overcome his current health limitations. Anthony is by nature dynamic, spontaneous, and optimistic.

Intellectually advanced at 15, I suspect that Anthony is among the best students in his class. He is organized and quick to grasp concepts, and he charges headlong into work and play.

At the same time, Anthony is not easy to live with. He expects a great deal from himself and from others. Although he is sociable, charming, and virile, he can be anxious, irritable, impatient, and selfish as well.

◆

Nick Is 15

Dear Anna,

I hope you are well, at 6.30 this morning, to hrd of the presidential election in . this was yesterday but nothing this morning, anyhow thats' about available news.

Love
From
Nick

Handwriting analysis:

- Strong, regular pressure: well-balanced, healthy boy.
- Small size: intelligence; virility; maturity.
- High upper stems: idealistic goals; vanity; high ambitions.
- Straight baseline: even tempered.
- Fast speed: intelligence, wit, quick mind.
- Slightly progressive slant: dynamic and ambitious.
- Wide spacing: need for independence; inner loneliness.
- Clear, connected script: respect for others, sociability.
- Strong, regular *t* crossings: willpower.
- Mostly full and closed lower loops: normal libido.
- Round and angular shape: intelligence; maturity; virility.
- Some end strokes launch upward: irritability; active temper.
- Lack of initial strokes: confident and uncritical; honest; can be gullible.

NICK'S PORTRAIT: The general aspect of this sample is extremely positive. While Nick displays the normal teenage ambivalences, he is emotionally and intellectually mature for his age. He has started dating and enjoys the company of girls.

Nick's goals are idealistic and high. He is an ambitious and dynamic scholar. At times he may feel a bit lonely intellectually. He is honest and trustworthy and thinks the best of other people. Nick may be rather vain. His script also reveals some inherent irritability and an active temper.

7

The Older Teenager
15 to 18

We are approaching the limits of childhood and adolescence. After 18 most teenagers can be considered young adults. However, real maturity is rarely achieved before the age of 23 and often much later.

As a matter of fact, personality development continues during the whole lifespan of an adult. Generally speaking, one's major character traits seem more stable after 23. The changeability of childhood and adolescence fades.

Between 15 and 18 the teenager's handwriting might deteriorate, depending on their reasoning capacities and maturity. Adjustments to their sex drives and needs for affection are not easy to achieve. The environment and surroundings have a decisive influence during this period. Teenagers are vulnerable and can be influenced easily. A first love can help to resolve most of the trials of puberty, or on the contrary, aggravate them.

Older teens long to live free, adventurous, or romantic lives, full of danger and excitement. At the same time, they lack sufficient maturity, physical strength, money, and other prerequisites to achieving these goals.

While girls mature earlier as a rule, many teenagers between 15 and 18 suddenly grow 2 to 3 inches all at once, within a few months. This puts a new perspective on things. A boy might be rather small during his childhood. The adults in his life are used to bending down to talk to him. Now they must look up to him. This oddity is both brutal and disturbing. Parents must learn to treat their kids like adults. A lack of respect toward youngsters at this age can be devastating.

By 18, adolescents are close to being grown-ups, and their handwriting analysis becomes more precise and less flexible than children's script. A persistently sinistrogyric slant at 18, for instance, is rather negative. At 15, this phenomenon is normal.

Handwriting analysis will reveal whether older teens' choices of coursework or future professions are adapted to their particular abilities. As their script becomes more stable, so do their gifts and drives.

Teenagers can, of course, be extremely stubborn and refuse to listen to any advice from parents. If that's the case, offer this book to your teenager. It can help to uncover latent gifts which he or she might want to develop. The tests at the end of the book will amuse older teens and can be useful in helping them to understand themselves. Above all, your own behavior and concept of life will be most valuable as an example to your teenager.

While you will never find two teenagers exactly alike, you will detect similarities in character. Since you must proceed by analogy as you progress in graphology, be on the lookout for samples. Compare them with the samples in this book. There is a good chance that you will find similar strokes among the samples—and similar personality traits among the writers.

152

Your skills are growing sharper. Therefore, the first sample in this chapter is the last to include a detailed handwriting analysis. In the remaining samples, I gradually reduce the detail and concentrate on the interpretation.

◆───────────────────◆

| **Samples** |

◆───────────────────◆

Nina, a Girl of 15

Handwriting analysis:

- Medium pressure: good physical health.
- Straight baseline: well-balanced child.

- Backward slant: common at this age; could indicate physical inhibition, dissemblance; selfishness; egocentric behavior.
- Inhibited script: inhibited, lacks spontaneity; good concentration; selfish.
- Open, tapered lower loops: destructive tendencies; unsatisfactory sexuality.
- Coils: selfish, egocentric; possible sexual acting out.
- Pronounced middle zone: realistic; materialistic.
- Altered letters: anxiety.
- Connected script: logical, good memory.
- Round shape: affectionate and feminine; artistic.
- Normal spacing: well-balanced girl.
- Ringlets: sociable; seductive or manipulative.

NINA'S PORTRAIT: This teenager is healthy, well balanced, and sociable. She is deep in the throes of adolescence, and her inhibitions and complexes will probably disappear when she reaches adulthood.

When she likes a task, she will concentrate and finish it; however, she prefers taking it easy and enjoying her leisure time. Nina lives in the present. She is artistically talented and has theatrical abilities as well.

♦

Neil Is a Boy of 15

Dear Dave,
        Thank you
very much for your last
letter. I enjoyed reading
it. This morning I watched
T.V. for half an hour,
and then I came to
school. I will see you
soon.

            Lots of
            Love

        Neil Coman

His writing is small and very fast; on a straight, regular baseline; with medium to strong pressure. This depicts intelligence, a quick and sharp mind, virility, and a maturity beyond the norm for his age-group.

The slant of Neil's writing is slightly variable, and there are some altered letters, which demonstrate his inner instability and anxiety. He is rather timid and not quite sure of himself. The spacing is wide, which reveals that he is very independent but sometimes a little lonely.

His intelligence and his vivacity will help him at college. He has great intellectual creativity.

◆

Mick Is a Boy of 15

I am
miss your lesson be
trip to the Hotel Nor
at 2 and will be returning just
ted I am sore gou will not nil
becoude you have never noticed I
see you some time

Best Wisher

Mick

Mick is physically healthy, but extremely inhibited and sexually ambivalent, which is not uncommon at his age (very round shape of letters; open lower loops in g and j). His thinking is slow (seen in his pasty, regular, and slow writing and backward slant).

Mick is rather lazy, and he has a great need for affection and immediate gratification (round letters in a pronounced middle zone of script, strong but pasty pressure). His lack of ambition is a problem for him (monotonous aspect of his writing; it is too regular and stiff). Mick is not very happy.

♦

Simon Is a Boy of 15

Dear Claude,

This morning I woke at 7:30 and then went to breakfast. I had cornflakes for breakfast and fried bread and baked beans. I then made a trip to the bicycle sheds.

Yours
sincerly

Simon is healthy and well balanced (strong, regular pressure; slightly variable slant is normal at his age). He is sociable and attached to his parents and his friends. His mind is analytical and deductive (regular, connected script). He is independent and sometimes a little lonely (wide spacing between words). He has respect for other people (easy-to-read script). He can be selfish and egocentric (lack of end strokes, backward slant).

Like Mick, Simon is sexually ambivalent (very round shapes and variable lower loops). This phenomenon is normal at his age and makes him feel slightly unsteady, timid, and depressed at times (baseline descending slightly).

He has a good imagination (high *i* dots), and he tries to do well at school. However, he is a slow learner and has little intuition (lack of disconnected strokes). I suspect that he gets better grades in mathematics than in literature.

◆

Heather Is a Girl of 16

Dearest Robin,
Well, here I
am writing from Gresha.
I had yummy cornflakes
for breakie, and then
History.
oodles of love
Heather.

Heather is extremely feminine and charming. Her health is good (medium, regular pressure). She has a great need for affection and gratification (very large and round script; pronounced middle zone).

Her mind is analytical and deductive but rather slow (slow writing, connected script). She has good intuition (some disconnected letters). Extremely selfish, she is able to manipulate others in order to get what she wants (lack of end strokes, arcades).

Her spontaneity is rather theatrical and put on (progressive slant; large, slow writing with arcades). She does not have much willpower or perseverance (lack of knotted loops and weak *t* crossings).

Heather has latent manual artistic talent and could become an actress, fashion model, painter, or decorator. Dancing or a professional activity linked with sports might also suit her.

She is not an intellectual. At school I imagine that she has some difficulties because she appears rather lazy and mainly interested in her physical appearance.

◆

Stephen Is a Boy of 16

Dear Mr. Haggie,

I hope you are well.
writing to you to inform you that i
next lesson, due to unforeseen source
apologie for the inconvenience.

y

Well-balanced and healthy (good pressure; regular, straight baseline; easy-to-read script), Stephen is intelligent, virile, and mature beyond the norm for his age-group (small and fast writing). He has a quick, sharp mind and a vivacious spirit.

Stephen is dynamic, active, ambitious, and hard working. He can show great passion for a chosen activity and finishes what he starts (very progressive slant, fast script, small size). His perseverance and willpower are strong (regular, straight baseline with strong *t* crossings; angular shapes).

In spite of his young age, he is comfortable with his sexuality (regular, strong, and closed loops in the lower zone; see *f* and *y* for instance). He is organized (regular spacing).

His intelligence and his passion for work will help him succeed in any field he chooses later on in life. He will probably be a brilliant student at college. He might become a doctor, journalist, lawyer, writer, or businessman.

◆

Chris Is a Boy of 16

16. Male.

Dear Claude,

I have just been kissed on the nose. The scientific name for a kiss is very long and only useful for Kissologists

Regards

Chris Boulz

Chris is healthy and well balanced. He is intelligent and has strong powers of concentration. He thinks before he acts. His mind is analytical and deductive (connected script, upright slant; regular script and spacing.) He lacks intuition (no disconnected strokes) and craves affection (round shapes).

He is very discreet and does not show his feelings (overlapping strokes, tight space between letters). He is stubborn. His libido (outlook on life, willpower, and sexuality) is not yet well developed. Chris is economically inclined and thrifty (tight spacing, small size). He can be selfish (lack of end strokes).

Chris might choose to become an accountant, lawyer, or civil servant. He does not mind routine activity and needs to be surrounded and encouraged by people. He is organized, punctual, and trustworthy.

♦

Rosie Is a Girl of 16

Dear William,

Missing you. Hope you're enjoying in Australia. Life's not terribly exciting The people are o.k. and everyone you know is fine. Nothing exciting is h. Hope to see you soon. Please write

Much love,

Rosie

Her handwriting depicts an intelligent and lively girl. Rosie is an optimist (fast and progressive script). She is dynamic, ambitious, and intellectually gifted. She may often feel bored or even irritable in class.

Rosie is moody, very independent, and sometimes a little lonely (variable slant and size of letters, wide spacing). She has an analytical, deductive mind and is very sociable (connected script). She can be perseverant (knotted loops in *t*'s), compliant, and generous (wide spacing and some end strokes in the letter *e* for instance).

REMEMBER: In these concise portraits we depict only the main personality characteristics which appear in the handwriting samples. The characteristics mentioned are more prominent in the person who wrote the sample than in the majority of other people in that age-group. If, for instance, I say that the teenager is selfish or intelligent or mature, I am comparing him or her to others at the same stage of development.

◆

James Is 16

Mrs Heggie,

This is just a short note to say there will be a meeting for all stage staff on monday afternoon to discuss the future of the drama department and the financial backing we intend to recieve.

yours

James is very intelligent and has a quick mind (fast script). His physical health is good (strong, regular pressure).

Emotionally, he is unstable, irritable, restless, and insecure. He wants to be independent but has difficulty assuming responsibility (altered letters; variable slant and size of script; covered strokes; ringlets; difficult to read.

James has an active temper. He's moody. He tries to hide his anxiety and inner distress by inventing stories and lying. He tries to please or manipulate adults in order to get what he wants (ringlets, round shapes).

His charm is rather feminine and his libido very ambivalent. This adds to his inner loneliness and anxiety (large spacing, altered letters, overlapping strokes).

◆

David Is 16

Hi Nic,

How are you? I don't suppose you're not having a good away from school, but I wonder if you ever miss it at all.

I can't write a long letter, as there isn't time, so I'll have to say goodbye.

Have a good Christmas,

love

(Male, 16 years old)

David is unusually intelligent and witty (fast and small script). At school he must be first in his class. He is very organized, punctual, and well balanced (regular, easy-to-read writing). He is economically inclined (tight, small letters).

David is principled and respects other people (stick-like upper stems). His perseverance and his willpower are strong (regular, short *t* crossings; some knotted loops and overlapping strokes). He is discreet, dynamic, ambitious, and masculine. His goals are high. At times he may feel lonely. He has some inhibitions.

David is more interested in studying and reading than in social events. He is independent, and he is selfish (small, tight script; reduced end strokes).

David's maturity is beyond the norm for his age group. I predict that he will become a brilliant college student and achieve his high, idealistic goals later on in life.

◆

Bill Is 16

Dear Lindsey,

Well I have to re write this letter because I've "lost" the first copy.

Basically I'm writing to tell you that the weather here is horrible & that I've got a cold, which means I haven't been able to run & swim.

Love

Physically and emotionally, Bill is rather fragile (very light pressure, variable slant, altered letters, irregular spacing). His manner is seductive; he likes to please others (ringlets). He is unhappy and rather lonely (large spacing).

Intellectually, Bill is beyond the norm for his age-group (small, fast script; round and angular shapes). He has a quick, sharp mind. Because he grasps concepts much more quickly than other pupils, Bill may feel bored at school. He is selfish (absence of end strokes) and restless.

Although he's emotionally unstable for his age, Bill's exceptionally high intelligence should enable him to earn any academic degree he sets his mind on.

◆

Bernard Is 17

Dear madame

The world we live in seems at odds with itself. It spins where I do not live. However we must be part of it that is our duty.

Yours faithfully

Bernard is very intelligent and has a vivacious spirit (small, fast, light script). He is virile (small script with normal lower loops and stems), but his physical health is rather fragile (light pressure). He must be doing well at school, for he appears very organized and well balanced. He does not blindly follow his impulses but thinks before he acts (backward slant).

He has a good imagination and may like to make up stories. He is selfish and not very trustworthy (lack of end strokes; light pressure; backward slant; his signature is very different from the handwriting of his message). He does not trust anyone very easily (superfluous dot after the signature). He can be arrogant and conceited (very pronounced upper zone in his signature).

♦

Freddy Is 17

Dear Claude,

*This morning d awoke se
times before d actually got u
d had spent a late evening c
a very good and filling suppl
(veal with spinach, tomato an*

He is intelligent, mature, well balanced and appears organized, reliable, hard working, dynamic, and healthy. Freddy's handwriting is extremely positive in every way. His letters are not altered, and there are no covered strokes. The spacing and the slant are regular.

He is sociable, perseverant and generous (round, connected script with ringlets and some knotted loops). His script is easy to reach, which implies respect for other people. His mind is critical, analytical, and deductive (long initial strokes; connected script).

Freddy is trustworthy and honest. He has a great imagination (high *i* dots, fast script). His libido is normal and virile (closed lower loops). Freddy will succeed in whatever career he chooses later on, as well as in his private life. He is happy, well adjusted, and feels responsible for his younger brothers and sisters.

◆

Suzy Is 17

> *Dear Duncan,*
>
> *Hi there old bean seeing rather a lot of you which is good because you mind and indeed you heard of things! Well I must have to get this special*

She is very feminine, charming, and quite happy (large, round, connected script with some garlands and ringlets. Suzy has a good imagination (high *i* dots) and a latent, manual artistic creativity (large, slow strokes). These features of her script also reveal that her need for affection and immediate gratification is strong. She can be selfish.

Her mind is analytical and deductive. Although she can sometimes show perseverance, generally she has difficulty getting organized and lacks concentration (altered letters, variable spacing, overlapping strokes; difficult-to-read script). She feels insecure.

Suzy is impatient, irritable, and may show arrogance toward other people (unfinished strokes; arcades; see the words "old" and "must," for instance). Suzy is moody and her health is rather fragile (variable pressure).

♦

Nicole Is 17

Dear Mother,

me, I'll be thinking about me & Simon, you always worry for no reason at all.

I'll be home soon and I'll bring you back a small gift. Tell dad, I'll send him something too.

Lots of love

Nicole Williamson.

Nicole is intelligent and has manual and intellectual abilities (medium speed, large script, strong pressure). She is healthy and well balanced. Her writing is easy to read, with regular spacing. Nicole has respect for other people. She is organized, dynamic, and ambitious (progressive slant, regular size).

Her mind is analytical and deductive; she is sociable, feminine, and charming (connected, round script). Her strong willpower can be seen in the straight baseline and the strong *t* crossings. She is independent but pleasant and compliant with her friends. She can be generous (a few end strokes).

Her libido is strong but still fluctuating (closed and open lower loops). Nicole is trustworthy and has a very positive handwriting and personality. She will succeed in life.

◆

Betty Is 18

shall show everyone. Mum and
photos - liked them. Looking foru
camping again with you rather th
sends you his love. Love you
I have just boiled at your ~~birthday~~
just get it! - I am abit slow.

Betty is healthy and well balanced but immature. Her
script is slow and seems too regular. Note the backward
slant and large, open lower loops. All this might be
normal at 14 or 15, but not at 18.

Betty is feminine and has a great need for affection
and gratification (round shapes), but at present she is
too selfish and lazy to build satisfactory relationships
with other people (no end strokes, disconnected script,
backward slant, overlapping strokes). She is very inhibited and egocentric for her age. She is unhappy and
feels lonely and frustrated (extremely wide spacing;
pronounced middle zone).

♦

Tara Is 18

Dear Claud,

this is my hand-writing. I
exatly know what to write, but I h
this little example of my hand writi
enough.

in an English
I am quite pleased

Tara is healthy, well balanced, and optimistic (strong pressure, regular script, ascending baseline). She knows how to manipulate others in order to get what she wants (arcades in *n* and *m*—these usually disappear by the age of 15 or 16). She is selfish (lack of endings).

Her mind is analytical and deductive but rather slow. She is not dynamic (slow, artificial script), but she is extremely organized. I fear that in spite of her ambitions, she will not achieve her intellectual goals. She is extremely lazy (slow, monotonous, childish script) and immature, and her intelligence is limited.

◆

Helen Is 18

sent me a bag
chocolate for my
journey to Montreal.

Let me tell you,
made my day.
Because leaving St.
and your Indian
feet, wasn't easy.

I'm heading for
but I'll be bac
Paris in a week.
I'll pop by to
hell.

Healthy and very lively, Helen usually follows her impulses and her whims. She appears to be a spendthrift (large, irregular size and spacing; long end strokes).

She is physical and cannot sit still for very long. Helen has some latent manual creativity (large script; pronounced middle zone). She can be spontaneous and dynamic (progressive slant), but she is not very trustworthy (altered letters; overlapping strokes; o made clockwise or of coils, which is unusual; jumbled script).

She is immature physically (distorted letters) and emotionally. Although Helen is very feminine and charming, her relationships with other people are stormy: she can be arrogant, very selfish, and bossy (convex t crossings, arcades).

♦

Martin Is 18

enclosed my autobiography - I stayed at
, August of this year but was unable
to fill I arrived home in Britain. I
to Jane who has been staying at
August (I'm afraid I can't remember
I'd be grateful if you could pass that
once she has already left could you please

He is organized, ambitious, and dynamic (fast, light, progressive script), but his physical and mental health are fragile (light, irregular pressure). He is well balanced and very organized. His mind is critical, analytical, and deductive. His goals are high. He is virile, and his libido is normal (long, closed lower loops).

Martin is perseverant and has willpower (knotted loops and strong, regular *t* crossings) and moral principles. At times he can be stubborn (sticklike stems), a little selfish, and inhibited. Generally he is sociable, tolerant, and compliant toward his friends.

♦

Nicole Is 18

Dear Claude

I'm glad that you aren't going to read this, I know I'd make many spelling mistakes

I love your shaker on the end of your chain, it is very pritty.

Thank you so much for coming today.

All my

Nicole feels sexually frustrated as a result of her physical and emotional immaturity. This is affecting her intellectual development (twisted, distorted strokes; open, distorted lower loops; backward slant; monotonous script).

She is very charming and feminine and needs affection and immediate gratification, which she may find in activities such as eating, going out with friends, and partying. I suspect that at school she is rather lazy and is not doing very well. She is very selfish (reduced end strokes).

◆

John Is 18

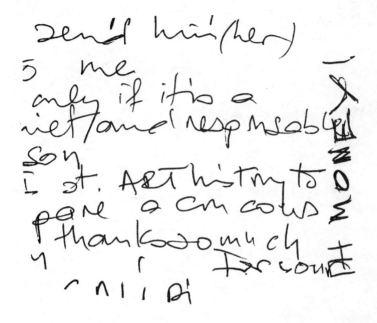

I consider John a borderline neurotic (extremely meandering baseline, jumbled script). He is anxious, untrustworthy, and confused (altered letters, covered strokes).
He is jumpy and cannot concentrate on any task for
very long. I suspect that John's parents always had
difficulties with their only son and that he displayed
mood swings and temper tantrums from an early age.
Today, John is very irritable, selfish, and conceited. He
is a spendthrift.

His parents, being wealthy, are able to fulfill his
ever-changing whims. Because of this, it's likely that he
never applied himself at school and has little interest in
choosing a profession.

♦

Louise Is 18

Dear Claude,

Howsit going?

Since you asked me, I sha tell you about my day! I got up at 10am and had a croissant for breakfast. I then over to the foyer to say goodby all my friends as I am leavin "Dublin" tonight. I also played

Her handwriting is very positive, like her character. Louise is trustworthy and loyal. Her maturity is beyond the norm for her age-group (small, fast, slightly irregular script; progressive slant; regular spacing). Her intellect and perseverance are strong (connected and disconnected script; round and angular shapes; knotted loops). She is sociable, charming, and feminine (ringlets).

Her willpower is strong (regular, short, and strong *t* crossings). She has a good imagination and latent intellectual creativity (high *i* dots; fast and slightly variable script). She can assume responsibility and her personality is strong. She is doing well at school. She might choose a career as a journalist, teacher, lawyer, doctor, or dentist.

PART THREE

PRACTICAL APPLICATIONS

8

Identifying Problems

At this point in your study of graphology, it will come as no surprise to learn that your children's drawings and handwriting can provide real clues—and cues—for gauging and responding to their overall well-being as well as to specific but transitory physical and emotional states. Children's graphics, like their personalities, are changeable. Each sample is a snapshot. Over time, collecting a set of samples provides an album that charts your child's developing personality.

As your child grows, you will gain insight into the general aspect of his or her development path. You'll be able to spot:

Changes, for example, growing independence as a toddler advances into childhood.

Trends, such as a child's basic disposition or general
   level of activity.
Blips, good days and bad days.
Traumas, from an accident, illness, or abuse.
Possible problems in physical, emotional, or intellec-
   tual development.

Remember always that your interpretations must
be flexible and tolerant and that your own emotions
and preoccupations will affect your children, for they
are tuned in to adults and are very intuitive. You will
learn to allow for the natural ebb and flow of a child's
developing personality, the ups and downs of everyday
life, and the effects that family history and environment
exert. As always, the general aspect of the sample depends on both the individual aspects such as pressure,
slant, and stroke *and* their interaction. Multiple samples will help you to interpret whether problems are
short-term, long-term, or tend to recur as a child grows
and changes.

Patterns of Development

The range of behavior that we may consider normal
among a group of children is wide. The following collection of graphics made by three children over a period of
time provides convincing evidence both of the range of
children's behavior at any age and of just how changeable they can be from one age to the next.

Simon

Scribbles at 4

Simon's scribbles reveal his contradictory feelings. He rebels against the authority of his parents. He's aggressive, temperamental, and probably cries easily. Note the strong pressure his his thick, dark (black) strokes and his choice of bright colors, blue and red. At the same time, Simon wants to please his parents (round strokes and ringlets). Such conflicts are common at 4.

◆

Simon's drawing at 5

He mainly depicts houses, which means that he is becoming more introverted, inhibited, and timid. He seeks his parents' protection and affection. I suspect that he is less temperamental but still moody. Simon is very charming (ringlets), but his feelings remain slightly contradictory (variable slant of his strokes and his houses).

Simon's writing at age 6

Like other young children, Simon's personality is jelling. His handwriting shows that his emotions are now well balanced. He is very intelligent: many children cannot write at this age. He tries to concentrate and do well. His spelling is correct, and he is perfecting his letters (covered strokes). The large spacing between his words reveals his growing need for independence.

a   boy   is   collecting
cookers   to   Play

◆

Ian

Scribbles at 4

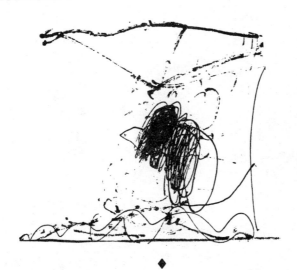

◆

Ian's drawings at 5

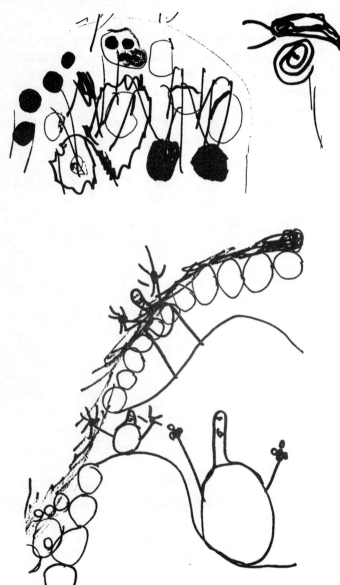

Ian is smart and has a great imagination. However, I suspect that he has difficulties getting along with other children. He may show aggressive behavior toward them or act shy and sulk in the corner. He's moody and irritable. None of this is uncommon between 4 and 6.

Emotionally, Ian is very nervous and at the same time inhibited. His drawings reveal his need for affection (many round shapes, ringlets, and coils) and his curiosity about sex. It's easy to pick up Ian's strong curiosity about sex (normal at this age). The sexual symbols are numerous all through his drawings. They depict both curiosity and fear (note that the hands of people in his drawings often look like claws). His anxiety is easy to sense in his scribbles as a 4 year old: the colors are black, bright red, and blue. Ian's strokes are fast, regular, and somehow monotonous. His pressure is too strong—almost violent like his colors.

Ian needs a consistent, nurturing environment in order to deal with his emotional fragility in the most positive ways.

◆

184

Ian's drawings at 5½.

The hands with claws and the large teeth in the last design reveal his anxiety and fear.

◆

Daisy

Daisy at 4

She is very intelligent and shows a talent for drawing. She's also very restless and temperamental. I suspect that, like Ian, she is rather aggressive toward other children but at the same time unsure of herself. Daisy's anxiety comes through in the violent colors (purple, orange, yellow, brown, and green); the strong monotonous pressure of the shadings; and the clawlike fingers of her figure. Daisy's animosity carries over into her relationships with other children and grown-ups.

Painting and drawing might drain off some of her restlessness and inner aggressiveness before she turns them inward. Like Ian, Daisy needs lots of guidance and love.

◆

Daisy's drawing at 6

Her emotions are balancing out. She is becoming more introverted and inhibited as she matures.

◆

Daisy's drawing at 7½

Her artistic talents are growing stronger. She is capable of concentrating on a chosen task, and her hostility is wearing off. Drawing has helped her.

◆

What to Look for in Drawings

Simon, Ian, and Daisy have shown us how children's personalities develop along individual paths. Signals that point to a psychological weakness most often are temporary. In those cases where a child's graphics mirror intense and prolonged suffering, proper care at the right time can help the child to regain confidence and become well balanced.

The General Aspect Is Fragmented

Disconnected strokes with no apparent relationship or meaning appear. The child uses only small portions of the paper, leaving large empty spaces.

Drawings of people often lack arms and hands. Children who are having problems with their parents or with brothers and sisters may draw these family members without faces or hands. Frightened children draw people with big teeth and long fingers.

Look for absurdities, for instance, a car with only one wheel or floating above the road like a helicopter.

Use of Color

Violent colors (bright red, purple, or black) appear frequently in drawings of troubled or nervous children, as do dull or drab colors (brown or gray). Colors convey a range of emotions and dispositions, from happy or optimistic to angry or depressed.

Pressure

Your interpretation of extreme heavy pressure will move away from "energy and general good health" to "suppressed emotions." Light pressure may signal a physically fragile child, a child with a soaring intellect, a nervous or restless child, or some combination of these traits.

In the case of children who have trouble controlling or expressing their emotions, the pressure may be spasmodic.

Monotony

Monotonous, repetitive strokes, usually with strong pressure, point to an artistic or creative child who is inhibited, timid perhaps, or sad. The child may be a problem eater. Here's a sample.

♦

Flatness

Flat drawings (that is, spread out horizontally) usually are the work of very young children or children who are young for their age-group. When a majority of a schoolchild's drawings are flattened, the child is expressing anxiety. It's similar to cats or dogs who flatten themselves on the ground when afraid. A sample:

Samples

Sharon Is 5

She says that her drawing represents the sea. Sharon's emotions are unstable. She is extremely restless, insecure, and impressionable. She may cry for no reason at all. She's moody, irritable, and doesn't eat well. She still wets her bed, and her parents are having trouble coping with her. You can sense the spasmodic pressure, which implies that Sharon has trouble controlling her emotions. Note, too, the monotonous strokes.

◆

Sophie Is 5½

I suspect that her family may be overprotective and too strict. Sophie's drawings show that she feels trapped and insecure, as illustrated by the person behind bars in her first drawing, the excessive size of the eyes and

mouths in the second drawing, and the monotonous strokes in the second and third drawings.

John Is 6

Extremely moody and irritable, John often bursts into tears without reason. He has a good imagination (both drawings float above the baseline) and a strong curiosity about sex (note the many sexual emblems in his drawings). I suspect that John is very restless, disobedient, and has difficulties concentrating. Emotionally he is both young for his age and fragile.

Thomas Is 6

Physically, Thomas seems quiet, apathetic, and weak. All his drawings are in one corner or on one side of the sheet of paper with a lot of empty space in the middle. The people he draws often have big hands but no faces. Perhaps his mother spoils her only child and watches very closely over all his activities. As a result, I suspect that Thomas is shy, inhibited, and uneasy around other children.

◆

Matthew Is 6

He is overactive and tries to drain off his excess energy.
Matthew's parents find him difficult to control. He is
stubborn, disobedient, moody, temperamental, and eats
poorly. His anxiety is acute: his drawing reveals his
inner violence.

♦

Fred Is 7

He cannot write yet, but his drawings show that he is very intelligent and imaginative. Unfortunately he is also irritable and has difficulty concentrating. Fred is extremely sensitive, and his health is fragile.

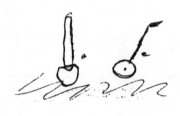

A Boy of 8

He is a slow learner but a hard worker. His father is an alcoholic, and this boy may have suffered a trauma of some sort as a younger child. He is moody and anxious; often his emotions are inappropriate. He writes and draws very slowly and bears down hard. Note the uncertain, altered letters and various sizes and slants in his printing.

◆

What to Look for in Handwriting

Here is a review of Glossary entries that are pertinent. Consult the Glossary for the full range of strokes and their interpretations.

Altered Script

Another sign of anxiety or insecurity. Remember, young children are simply perfecting their letters. In the script of older children, altered strokes may indicate moodiness, emotional instability, immaturity, or irresponsibility.

Baseline (Disposition)

The baseline may meander, along with the child, into adolescence. Disposition, overall level of activity, and maturity all affect the baseline. An extremely meandering baseline showing a very light pressure may indicate an acute problem, such as a temporary illness or emotional upset, or long-term emotional instability. If the baseline is usually straight and suddenly, one day, it plunges downward, the child probably doesn't feel well.

Distorted (Twisted) Script

A sign of illness, distorted strokes are normal and temporary in adolescents with active hormones; could indicate thyroid problem.

Extremely Variable Slant within the Same Sentence or Word

Usually this characteristic is transitory. If it's persistent into the late adolescence, an extremely variable slant signals an emotionally unstable, nervous, or restless person.

Jumbled Script

Letters and lines flowing into each other signal mental confusion or possible substance abuse.

Monotonous Script

A normal aspect of children's handwriting up to adolescence, monotony in an older teen's script may signal a temporary regression back to a younger behavior pattern, or it may point to a neurotic tendency.

Overlapping (Covered) Strokes

Anxiety, depression, eating problems.

Pasty Script

Laziness, self-absorption, sexual fantasies.

Pressure Is Light or Spasmodic

As described in the section on drawings, children who have trouble expressing or controlling their emotions may have a spasmodic pressure. Very light pressure may signal anxiety, poor health, or physical changes.

A teenager who displays spasmodic pressure might be using drugs. If you see this in combination with other signs, start asking questions.

Samples

Dominic Is 7

Note Dominic's altered letters and shaky, unfinished strokes. His lower loops seem to be hanging down limply into the line below. The size and slant of his letters are variable, and the spacing is wide. His drawing has a monotonous aspect.

Dominic likes to be alone. He seeks seclusion and refuses to play or even talk with other children. Emo-

tionally he is very sensitive—a trait that is highlighted by his intuitive nature—and easily depressed. Physically he is fragile.

♦

Mark Is 10

Mark is in therapy because he is practically uncontrollable. He feels confused and insecure. His writing is difficult to read. It is jumbled, with altered letters of various sizes and numerous overlapping strokes. The great variability of the pressure in his strokes is a function of Mark's constant anxiety and emotional instability. He is very sensitive and fragile.

Wine The poo woke op sudden of the night and listened

was a goat named Gregory c np from rock to rock kick his legs i Butt his head against wall goat said Gregory

♦

Martin Is 13

His monotonous writing is the first clue to Martin's inhibited nature. Note also the backward slant, tight letters, and the way he dots his *i*'s. Martin lacks spontaneity. He is unable to express his thoughts and feelings and finds it hard to cope with life. He's insecure and has a poor relationship with his parents. Martin wishes he was a little boy again.

Today I went signed myself in and went up to the hatch. I didn't like the hot food. went to the toaster and got two hot toast. I then went to the tab I talked alot with my friends or them questions about yesterday.

♦

A Girl of 16

In all her samples, the baseline is plunging downward. She is chronically depressed and also physically fragile.

this morning,
maths. I've

afternoon I
get Physics and Chemistry. On Sunday I'm
doing a military parade through
Hold to its war memorial for
Remembrance Sunday.

Marcus W...R

REMEMBER: If the baseline in your child's samples is normally straight and then suddenly slants downward, the child probably doesn't feel well.

♦

Marcus Is 16

Intelligent but mentally fragile, Marcus cannot concentrate or make decisions. Nothing he begins ever gets finished. His fast, small, connected script reflects intelligence, but his anxiety and emotional instability is revealed in the altered letters and the varying slants, sizes, and shapes of his strokes as well as in the meandering baseline. Note that his *a*'s and *t*'s, for instance, show a half dozen shapes within this small sample.

I suspect that Marcus is untrustworthy and tries to hide his real feelings. His difficulties certainly must reflect on his schoolwork. All in all, he's not a happy teenager.

Dear Nemone,

Thanks for your letter. Morning lessons were very boring. German was a shag and French was boring Please write soon

Love

Anne

♦

Diana Is 17

She's been in treatment for psychotic behavior for many years. Note the context of Diana's sample. The numerous tapered strokes show her strong self-destructive tendencies. The pressure is variable and combines with the varying shapes of her block letters to reveal her lack of self-control.

♦

Fred Is 17

Fred became addicted to heroin at the age of 15 and refuses to seek help. His mind is altered. The handwriting of drug addicts often shows aspects similar to the script of those who suffer from severe psychological disorders. Note the heavy pressure—too strong to be natural.

in those places____; listen,
ask for another allfat—once,
breakfast in return.
nurse! no cigarettes!
endless excuses 2 laugh
future. As it is America
the barnyard. Remark!

♦

Danny Is 18

More than two years of cocaine abuse has left its mark on Danny. Basically he is intelligent (small, fast, connected script), but his intellectual abilities, including his memory, are slowly deteriorating. Most of his letters are altered and difficult to read. Their sizes are variable as is the pressure. Note the shaky *i* dots.

Hey Wig, what the hell are you doing in London, when I'm here ??? Oh well, I just hope you'll be here next time! if Not, see you in Laguna Beach December 1986

Luv Dan

◆

Neil Is 18

The ringlets and the round shapes point to a strong ambivalence in this teenager's libido. He's probably not sure whether he prefers girls or boys. The long lower loops, plunging into the line below, also indicate excess physical energy. Neil needs to move around a lot. Physical exercise helps him work off his energy.

Neil keeps changing his goals and moving on to new activities without ever finishing anything he starts. He is in psychotherapy, which helps him to cope with his inner confusion, emotional instability, and insecurity. These traits are evident in Neil's jumbled and altered letters, embellished script, numerous overlapping strokes, and meandering baseline

♦

Jacky Is 18

Intellectually, Jacky is performing at the level of the average 12 year old. Her physical health is precarious, and she's endured various physical ailments throughout her youth. Her incapacitation, evident in the numerous twisted letters in the upper, middle, and lower zones, has kept her out of school for months at a time, which contributes to her slow mental development.

9

Testing Your Skill

Sample Test 1

General Personality Traits of Children

You do not need to see a great amount of handwriting to get some idea of a child's basic character traits. Avoid photocopies because you can't evaluate the pressure. Remember that the sample should be spontaneous. Your interpretation of a passage copied from a book or written from dictation will be unreliable. In the following exercise, each sample reveals mainly one specific character trait. Choose the correct one.

1. This adolescent girl is

(a) ☐ spontaneous.

(b) ☐ seductive.

(c) ☐ inhibited.

not interested in this. Did the watch, I am so gave it to you - since

♦

2. This boy is

(a) ☐ charming and feminine.

(b) ☐ lazy.

(c) ☐ hard working and cruel.

That has interested. People. Maybe we can.

♦

3. For her age, this girl of 15 is

(a) ☐ mature.

(b) ☐ immature.

(c) ☐ inhibited.

her surname) and I wrote on to her. If by any ch nail it to her address

♦

4. This girl is

(a) ☐ in good physical health.

(b) ☐ feeling ill.

(c) ☐ mentally fragile.

wife & daughter been in, now.

◆

5. This 13-year-old girl is

(a) ☐ well balanced.

(b) ☐ emotionally unstable.

(c) ☐ untrustworthy.

could get. later, he the University of geor. of many failures, he his experiments. In 1773

◆

6. This boy of 7 is

(a) ☐ well balanced.

(b) ☐ mentally fragile.

(c) ☐ inhibited.

a litte ber was a monts apiyd in manster

◆

7. This girl of 13 is

(a) ☐ very intelligent.

(b) ☐ a slow learner.

(c) ☐ very ambitious.

fun. I play lots y and cross say is it looks as

♦

8. This boy of 18 is

(a) ☐ well balanced and healthy.

(b) ☐ using drugs.

(c) ☐ artistic.

WIG, you are in DEEP SHIT Thumb & I are here, but you're in fucking England!

♦

9. This 12-year-old boy is

(a) ☐ timid and introverted.

(b) ☐ spontaneous and happy.

(c) ☐ physically fragile.

Dear Claude,

♦

10. This boy of 13 is

(a) ☐ mentally fragile.

(b) ☐ temperamental.

(c) ☐ moody.

time in

soon, where

live? I live

13 years old.

Solutions

1. (c) Slow writing; pasty aspect; open and large loops in the lower zone; common during adolescence.

2. (c) Fast, angular script; tapered endings; the original reveals strong pressure.

3. (a) Fast, small script; slightly meandering baseline; medium pressure.

4. (b) Distorted script; baseline descending.

5. (a) Regular size and shape; straight baseline; slightly backward slant, normal at this age; pressure and speed are medium.

6. (b) Irregular pressure and size; variable slant; irregular shapes; irregular spacing; bad spelling.

7. (b) Extremely slow writing; monotonous aspect; arcades.

8. (b) Irregular shapes; altered letters; variable pressure; meandering baseline; tapered strokes; odd context.

9. (b) Progressive slant; fast script; regular pressure and shapes; fairly straight baseline.

10. (c) Variable slant and spacing.

SCORING: Give yourself 5 points for each correct answer:
40–50 = Excellent
30–40 = Good
20–30 = Average
10–20 = Poor
0–10 = Review the Glossary and the chapters which cover the age-groups you interpreted incorrectly.

Sample Test 2

Interpreting Children's Drawings

1. This 11-year-old girl is

(a) ☐ happy and well balanced.

(b) ☐ sad.

(c) ☐ trustworthy.

◆

2. This boy of 8 is

(a) ☐ healthy and happy.

(b) ☐ fragile and inhibited.

(c) ☐ boisterous.

◆

3. Most likely, this boy of 7

(a) □ has temper tantrums.

(b) □ is extremely interested in sex.

(c) □ has an excessive need for affection.

4. At 10, this girl is

(a) ☐ intelligent and mature for her age.

(b) ☐ seductive and manipulative.

(c) ☐ emotionally unstable.

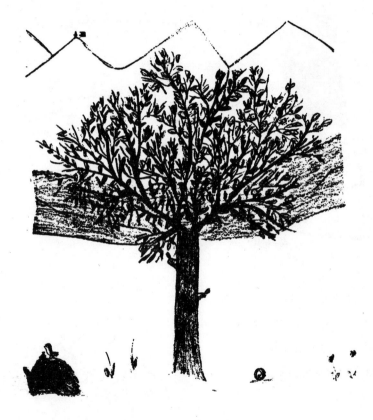

5. This boy of 8 is

(a) ☐ healthy and well balanced.

(b) ☐ mentally fragile.

(c) ☐ feeling ill.

◆

6. This little girl of 7 has

(a) ☐ intellectual abilities.

(b) ☐ artistic gifts.

(c) ☐ manual talents.

◆

7. This 10-year-old girl's main abilities are

(a) ☐ verbal.

(b) ☐ manual.

(c) ☐ mathematical.

◆

8. For his age, this boy of 7 is very

(a) ☐ intelligent and mature.

(b) ☐ aggressive.

(c) ☐ unstable.

TO munɵo
love
saffron

◆

9. At 6, this boy is

(a) ☐ fragile, unstable.

(b) ☐ calm and well balanced.

(c) ☐ manipulative.

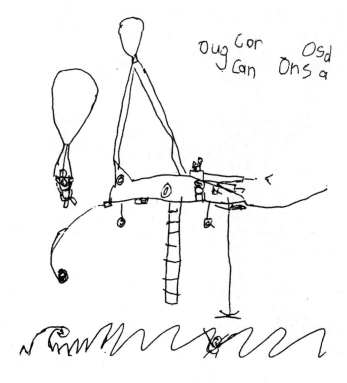

10. This girl of 5 has

(a) ☐ a psychological disorder.

(b) ☐ excellent physical and mental health.

(c) ☐ intellectual ability.

Solutions

1. (a) See Example 2.1, page 28.
2. (b) Lack of face and hands.
3. (b) Lots of sexual emblems.
4. (a) Note the composition and proportion.
5. (b) Variable pressure; monotonous strokes; fragmented aspect.
6. (c) Large hands; proportion, detail.
7. (c) Numerous rectangular shapes.
8. (a)

9. (a)

10. (a)

SCORING: Give yourself 5 points for each correct answer: 40–50 = Excellent
30–40 = Good
20–30 = Average
0–20 = Review especially Chapters 2–5.

Sample Test 3

Adolescent Development and Aptitude

1. At 12, this young girl has

(a) ☐ a great need for affection.

(b) ☐ a virile, tough character; she is rather cruel.

(c) ☐ an ambitious and dynamic personality.

ou like this, pen to paper, feelings
ner, I hear you cry us your
er breakfast and you glare
it.

2. This girl of 18 is

(a) ☐ sociable and polite.

(b) ☐ slightly arrogant.

(c) ☐ nasty and stubborn.

about your bookshop in
and I was wondering if
are any temporary posts
. I have worked as a sales
Smith in Stafford for two

◆

3. This boy of 15 is

(a) ☐ sad.

(b) ☐ well balanced.

(c) ☐ neurotic.

a major port in a
picture . I do believe
ill come as good

All the best —

◆

4. This boy of 15 has

(a) ☐ poor physical health.

(b) ☐ a psychological disorder.

(c) ☐ constant mood swings.

[handwritten text:]

> with work
> down to Breakfast
> friend.
>   After breakfast
> a game of pool. I
>   Yours
>   Sincerly.

♦

5. This teenager is

(a) ☐ sexually ambivalent.

(b) ☐ depressed.

(c) ☐ pessimistic.

[handwritten text:]

> Duncan Cargill (me)
>   Well hello Claude,
> Mrs Whit has told me so mn
> about you. My ambition
> is to (be) an au pair for th
> French president and the
> shoot him

♦

6. At 16, this boy's sexual orientation appears

(a) ☐ heterosexual.

(b) ☐ homosexual.

(c) ☐ ambivalent.

The quick
fox jumped
the easy

Keiro

◆

7. This boy of 17 is

(a) ☐ spontaneous and charming.

(b) ☐ inhibited and vengeful.

(c) ☐ generous and hard working.

Dear Claude,

How are
you, I'm fine. This
morning has been
very relaxing. I've had
a double study and

◆

8. A primary trait of this 17-year-old boy's personality is

(a) ☐ intelligence.

(b) ☐ vanity.

(c) ☐ generosity.

Dear Claude,

Yet another day in a world. Still it's not so bad, The crosswords, my art, (above what the hell am I talki. glad, you've come to Gres

♦

9. This boy of 14 is rather

(a) ☐ intellectual.

(b) ☐ mature.

(c) ☐ spoiled.

How's life. The weather
and pretty hopeless really.
lish lesson that we are
~ is most thrilling and

♦

10. This boy of 16 has abilities for

(a) ☐ sports.

(b) ☐ academics.

(c) ☐ mechanics.

well I had a really
fancinating morning, what
with getting up and getting
washed and no on, well
you know how it is!

Solutions

1. (a) Extremely round shapes; large, round, and open loops in the lower zone.

2. (b) Note the arcades, which appear mainly in the *o*'s and are made with clockwise strokes (going backward). In older adolescents and adults, arcades signal vanity and arrogance, deceit, and/or manipulative behavior.

3. (a) Descending baseline and wide spacing between words.

4. (c) Variable slant and altered letters.

5. (a) Large and odd-shaped lower loops which fall into the next line.

6. (b) Extremely round handwriting; large script; full upper and lower loops. The script seems blown up.

7. (b) Backward slant; regressive, angular strokes mainly in the lower loops; endings going backward.

8. (b) Extremely high, sticklike stems.

9. (c) Slow, round, and childish script; arcades.

10. (a) Long, full loops in the lower zone; large script; pronounced middle and lower zone.

SCORING: Give yourself 5 points for each correct answer:
40– 50 = Excellent
30– 40 = Good
20– 30 = Average
below 20 = Review Chapters 5, 6, and 7.

CONCLUSION

♦

If you have studied the samples in this book carefully, you are now capable of analyzing and interpreting the drawings and handwriting of children and adolescents. Graphology can reveal precise details about a child's personality, daily behavior and experiences, and developmental pattern. Drawings and handwriting divulge latent talents and aptitudes.

You will be able to tell whether your children are basically well balanced and happy; to identify problems, insecurities, or anxieties; and to judge which situations are temporary and age-appropriate and which may need attention.

Scribbles, doodles, and drawings will reveal restlessness and instability in children from the age of 2 up. Keeping track of their graphics will help you monitor what's happening while they are in the care of others. In combination with your observations of an older child's physical and mental growth pattern, you may be able to identify aberrations in behavior—such as early drug or alcohol use—by keeping track of changes in his or her handwriting.

Bring a degree of tolerance and a heaping measure of flexibility to your interpretations of young people's graphic expression, for children change and grow before our eyes. And remember that drawing is good therapy for anyone at any age.

Enjoy your new-found skill!